'INTO ANOTHER MOULD'
ASPECTS OF THE INTERREGNUM

This is a second, revised and enlarged edition of a pioneering book originally published by University of Exeter Press in 1981.

The opening chapter by Ivan Roots, 'Unity and Disunity in the British Isles' has been recognised as a ground breaking essay on the British dimension of the civil war and Interregnum. Stephen Roberts' survey, 'Local Government Reform in England and Wales during the Interregnum', stresses the preoccupation of legislators and administrators with security and finance. Dr Roberts has also written a new chapter for this edition, on developments in Wales; the Principality is too often overlooked as a distinct entity and too readily subsumed into England-and-Wales. Another major aspect is contemplated by Peter Gaunt in a fresh examination of Cromwell's relations with his parliaments, vital in both the constitutional and political history of the 1650s. The final chapter, 'The Politics of the Army and the Quest for Settlement' by Derek Massarella, brings together two pervasive themes, emphasising how a crisis of identity in the New Model Army, extending from 1645 to 1660, brought about the Restoration which it could not prevent and to which, in the event, it contributed.

GW00656800

The cover illustration is taken from a reproduction of
The Great Seal of the Commonwealth of England.

Exeter Studies in History
General Editors: Jonathan Barry, Tim Rees and T.P. Wiseman

Also in the Exeter Studies in History series:

*From Deliverance to Destruction: Rebellion and
Civil War in an English City*
Mark Stoyle (1996)

*Witchcraft in Early Modern Scotland: King James'
Demonology and the North Berwick Witches*
Lawrence Normand and Gareth Roberts (forthcoming)

'INTO ANOTHER MOULD'
ASPECTS OF THE INTERREGNUM

Edited by
IVAN ROOTS

UNIVERSITY
of
EXETER
PRESS

First published in 1981 by
University of Exeter Press
Reed Hall, Streatham Drive
Exeter, Devon EX4 4QR
UK

New edition, revised and expanded, 1998

British Library Cataloguing in Publication Data
A catalogue record for this book is available from the British Library

ISBN 0 85989 417 7

Typeset in 10/12pt Sabon by Kestrel Data, Exeter

Printed in Great Britain by
Short Run Press Ltd, Exeter

Contents

Preface to the Revised Edition

'*Into Another Mould*' (1998) is the second, enlarged and somewhat revised edition of one of the earliest volumes in the proliferating Exeter Studies in History series. The original articles appear to have stood the test of time. The new contributions, broadening the scope of the 'aspects of the Interregnum', emphasise the appeal and significance of a period sometimes described as 'a long inevitable anti-climax' from the execution of Charles I and the abolition of monarchy to the Restoration of 1660. Nothing, of course, is inevitable and the developments of the 1650s deserve critical attention in their own right.

The editor, acutely conscious of his own part in the elephantine gestation of this volume, is grateful to his contributors for their patience as well as their expertise. Equally, he expresses heartfelt thanks to the University of Exeter Press Editorial Panel and to Simon Baker, Richard Willis and the staff of University of Exeter Press for their unfailing courtesy and co-operation. Now the book must make its own way in the world.

Ivan Roots, 1998

Notes on Contributors

PETER GAUNT is head of the Department of History at Chester College and Chairman of the Cromwell Association. He is the compiler of *The Cromwellian Gazetteer* (1987) and author of *Oliver Cromwell* (1995).

DEREK MASSARELLA is Professor of History at Chuo University, Tokyo. His *A World Elsewhere* (1990) contemplates Europe's encounters with Japan in the sixteenth and seventeenth centuries.

STEPHEN ROBERTS is editor of the 1640–1660 section of *The History of Parliament*. His *Recovery and Restoration in an English County: Devon Local Administration 1646–1670* was published by University of Exeter Press in 1985.

IVAN ROOTS is Emeritus Professor of History at the University of Exeter and past President of the Cromwell Association. He wrote *The Great Rebellion 1642–1660* (5th edn 1995) and edited *Speeches of Oliver Cromwell* (1990).

Peter Gaunt and Stephen Roberts are former postgraduate students of the editor and Derek Massarella studied as an undergraduate with him.

Introduction to the Revised Edition

Ivan Roots

The Interregnum is commonly defined as the period between the abolition of monarchy in 1649, following the public execution of Charles I, and the recreation of that institution in the person of Charles II in 1660. A useful term certainly, it is also somewhat misleading, hinting as it does that the eleven years of unkingly rule were a mere aberration, to be swept aside by an ultimately irresistible pressure to return to the old, even natural, order. Such a view, inhibiting a proper examination of years more eventful and more exciting than that other decade, the 1630s of Charles I's so-called personal rule, should be resisted. This second, revised and enlarged edition of '*Into Another Mould*' (initially published in 1981) takes up some major aspects worthy of independent investigation, each related to what was the prime objective of the regimes of the Interregnum—the search for a settlement of the issues out of which the civil wars of the 1640s had emerged and those which had emerged out of the civil wars.

The search had already set off even before war started 'formally' in August 1642. What was at stake throughout England (and Wales) was relevant to what had happened in Scotland (certainly since 1637) and in Ireland (since 1641), each a main constituent of Charles I's multiple inheritance. These relations, in which the King himself was the most prominent element, merged into a British civil war, in which there were always more than two sides. Negotiations pursued throughout the war settled nothing. Parliament's military victory, won by 1646 by its New Model Army, settled nothing. Indeed, settlement was made more remote as army and parliament drifted apart and a stubborn Charles I stuck to his divide-and-rule campaign to make himself 'King again'. 'Stone dead' had been Essex's solution to the problem of Strafford in 1641. By 1649 for the army and those who remained in the Commons after Pride's Purge 'stone dead' was the necessary prelude to a continuing hunt for certainty. The Interregnum began with nothing positive resolved.

The Commonwealth began on an *ad hoc* basis. It has been commonly described as a stop gap, an expedient rather than an experiment, though there is currently an effort, which deserves some consideration, to demonstrate determined moves to 'invent' a republic, with principled practices.[1] Be that as it may, the new regime found from the start it had to take arms (the New Model) against a sea of problems, not only in England, but across 'the British Isles', whose purely dynastic unity had dissolved as Charles I's head fell from his shoulders, and from overseas, where reports of regicide made monarchs gingerly finger their collars. It was quickly apparent that the new regime could not afford to let the British Isles fragment, and that there were those in both Scotland and Ireland who would not welcome such an alteration. In all three countries an urge to stop the rot became a central fact in the search for a settlement.

So in late 1649 Oliver Cromwell, 'chief of men' not only for Milton, set the reconquest of Ireland going with a swift, brutal and effective campaign. His triumph prompted the composition (though not the publication) of Andrew Marvell's remarkable political *Horatian Ode*. Subtle in its comments on the immediate past, the Ode was also prophetic. Cromwell was in the process of casting 'the kingdoms old / Into another mould'. No one else could do that. Marvell went on to predict that 'the same arts' that had gained 'a power must it maintain'. One such art was the sword which 'for the last effect' must still be kept erect. By the spring of 1654 Cromwell's frustration with that situation was apparent and the history of the Protectorate and its aftermath demonstrates a mission to make 'a firm state'—another Marvellian echo—not just in England but across the three constituent countries, in a composite state, no longer loosely kingly, but tighter in unity. The means to bring that about were diverse—by military conquest, by formal unification under a written constitution, embracing (rather fictitious) Scots and Irish representation in an imperial parliament, by the Prince of Wales's co-operation sought between particular groups in both islands and by vigorous denial of opportunities for a comeback. Each of the articles in this collection tackles an aspect of that protracted search for stability.

'Union and Disunion' provides a 'British' context for the 1650s, looking back a little. Like 'Interregnum', 'British' has more utility than validity. It is hard to find an agreed definition for it. It is rather like the experience of the USA in the middle of this century when it was easier to demonstrate what was *un*-American than what was positively American. Nowadays Irish historians reject it but when they write about the broader context for their own country they find alternative terms hard to come by. (The existence of 'Northern Ireland' does not help.)[2] The fact is England (with Wales), Scotland, Ireland, to say nothing of the Channel Islands, the Orkneys and the Isle of Man, were flung together in these years into a peculiar relationship, in fact Marvell's 'another mould', which produced, however temporarily, a sort of entity within which there was for England an ascendancy, which would survive. But both Ireland and Scotland were also marked by the way things went for them under Commonwealth and Protectorate. Wales, too.

In the application of a British dimension to the events of the 1640s and 1650s, Wales tends to get overlooked—as, indeed, it is in 'Union and Disunion'. The explanation for the omission is complex. It is not enough to say that Wales was small in size and thin in population, poverty-stricken and remote. More important, it lacked, and had long lacked, what Ireland and Scotland had—separate existence as (more or less) discrete entities. When was Wales? asked Gwyn A. Williams, surveying the centuries.[3] Certainly not in the Middle Ages, and hardly since. Some might say that only when the Welsh Assembly of limited devolution meets will a genuine Wales come into a fragile being, one which no doubt for its continuance must demand yet more devolution. Stephen Roberts asserts in 'Religion, Politics and Welshness, 1649–1660' that the Wales incorporated into England under Henry VIII 'was not a kingdom, not even a state, but an ill-defined territory assimilated' into a larger unit. Yet for all that there was something which could be called 'Welshness', which showed and still shows a remarkable capacity for survival. Roberts sets out to see how that quality of Welshness was affected by the experience of Commonwealth and Protectorate. His consideration is based largely on the Rump's major innovation across Offa's Dyke: the Commission for the Propagation of the Gospel in Wales, regarded as very much 'a dark corner of the land'. The commission's bustling, even radical, activities, continued on a somewhat different footing as 'triers' and 'ejectors' during the Protectorate, made it seem 'the real government of Wales', 'the very dynamic', involved from the outset in things secular as well as spiritual, where a dividing line ran erratically. Even so, the normal machinery of Wales's government—including courts and constables—though disturbed in the war years was coming back, a token of acceptance of Cromwellian rule. Roberts argues that the commissioners initially saw themselves as 'the agents of a victorious English parliament'. Yet they were mostly Welsh. Among them there was a hint of Welshness, particularly in Morgan Llwyd, prophetic promoter of a Welsh cultural identity, addressing himself in both Welsh (mostly) and English to the Welsh peoples, whom he regarded as having had 'a distinguished and special past'. Roberts also brings in William Erbery, not a commissioner, but an itinerant preacher, a South Walian (unlike Llwyd, who came from the North) without fluency in Welsh. What Erbery had was a sense of a Welsh destiny within a Britain, including Scotland, where 'the glory of God will first be manifest'. Wales was not, could not be, isolated from what was going on elsewhere—and Wales, the Welsh (some of them, at least, like Colonel John Jones the Regicide) and Welshness had their own external impacts, an aspect yet to be thoroughly explored.

Wales crops up again in Roberts's earlier innovative article on 'Local Government Reform under the Commonwealth and Protectorate', re-printed here with a bibliographical update. Evaluation of a local dimension for the causes and progress of the civil war began to appeal to historians of various outlooks during the 1950s, and, as Roberts's introductory commentary on 'Civil war historians and the government of localities' testifies, has since proliferated. What has come to be called 'localism' has taken up many themes, prominent among them the relationship between central and local interests, in that stress has been put 'more on personnel than on structure, more on participation than on performance', with insufficient attention paid to the actual institutions involved. Roberts, however, concerns himself with these, particularly during the Interregnum, a decade which in even some of the best local studies has been rather perfunctorily treated—half-a-dozen chapters, say, on 1640–49, and but one each to the 1650s and to the collapse of 1659–60. For his part Roberts begins with 1647 and the constitutional proposals of the Levellers and of the army grandees, which centred directly and indirectly on local issues. The Levellers were the more enterprising as 'the only political thinkers of the English Revolution' to come up with 'a notion of "local government" as a basis of political change', though certainly similar ideas would be put forward under different auspices during the 1650s, notably among law reformers. None of this amounted to setting up a distinct 'local government' lobby, but it can be claimed that there was something like a corpus of Interregnum legislation—acts and ordinances and a mass of *ad hoc* innovations, such as the appointment of local bodies of commissioners to work with the major-generals, all of whom significantly wanted to be JPs. Their instructions show clearly how the administration of social and economic legislation was an integral part of the 'healing and settling' process, yet never quite detached from the overwhelming demands of security, which both advanced and retarded the return to 'normalcy', the ultimate *desideratum* for an ageing Cromwell looking back to his civilian roots.[4]

The constitutional history of the Interregnum is largely parliamentary. The House of Lords, found by experience, mostly recent, as 'useless and dangerous', was abolished along with the monarchy. (The peerage *per se* remained.) But the Commonwealth was based upon the continuance of a purged (but later slightly augmented) House of Commons, indeed initially upon the unhesitant preservation of the existing House, to the point that Cromwell could later argue plausibly that it intended to perpetuate itself, protected as it was by the statute of 1641 allowing dissolution solely by its own consent. (But should the single-chamber Rump really be equated with the parliament that was assembled in 1640?) The Keepers of the Liberties of England were determined to do things in 'a parliamentary way'. So traditional officials carried on and procedures for debates, legislation and committees were unchanged. A Great Seal (though to a new pertinent design) was retained. The uniquely respected position of Speaker was observed. Even so, when in April 1653 Cromwell as Lord General forcibly dissolved the Rump, he did not say that henceforth there would be no parliaments but denounced this one as 'no parliament'.[5] The subsequent Nominated Assembly transformed itself into a parliament, elected a Speaker and did what it did according to the old rituals. Into the Instrument of Government a single-chamber parliament was put as essential to the written constitution. The Protector would claim later that it was, with the Single Person, 'a fundamental'. If the Council of State was 'the key to the constititution', Cromwell's calling of two parliaments points to a genuine desire to work with the traditional institution, though in a somewhat novel form. His own parliamentary history, which began in 1628, hardly justifies the jibe that he was 'a mere back-bencher', ignorant of the variety of purposes parliaments had evolved to fulfil. The second Protectorate Parliament saw a revival of a second chamber, 'the other House', which immediately took upon itself the officials and procedures, and, its critics suspected, the claims of the old upper chamber. The third Protectorate Parliament (Richard's) was called upon historical franchises and (as reported in impressive detail in Burton's *Diary*)[6] was unhesitant in its implementation of the old rules, dominated as it was by men like Sir Arthur Hesilrige, who between 1640 and 1653 had mastered the parliamentary arts and looked back to the Commonwealth as golden years. Notably the Protectorate parliaments concerned themselves with private as well as public legislation, as parliaments have done before and since. If the first so-called 'eleven years tyranny' of 1629–40 was notorious for its lack of parliaments, the second of 1649–60 was a plethora of them. Novel they were, yet as Peter Gaunt confirms in his thoughtful survey of Cromwell and his parliaments, they were in many ways, large and small, typical of the assemblies of the seventeenth century.

Gaunt tackles the classic Trevor-Roper thesis, so dismissive of the parliamentary skills of Oliver and his government.[7] Brisk and brilliant, Trevor-Roper performed something of a conjuring trick. Gaunt, who has additionally thoroughly researched the protectoral Councils of State, is more thorough and more convincing in a balanced survey, which groups Cromwell's relations with parliament under three heads: 'co-operation, conflict and control'. There is material and argument to Cromwell's credit under them all, with rather more under the second head in the first parliament than in the second assembly, certainly in the latter's first session. Gaunt deploys all this not simply in a negative approach to Trevor-Roper; indeed, there is much in the latter's detail that he is inclined to accept, but he rejects the portrayal of these two parliaments as out-and-out failures. He sees a positive side to the aspirations and activities of Protector and MPs alike. Certainly, some efforts 'were unsuccessful or half-hearted, but business was conducted, legislation prepared [and passed] and the ship of state was kept afloat'. Perceptively Gaunt emphasises that these parliaments of the 1650s reflected 'the politics of division and novelty which had pervaded parliamentary politics since 1640, if not before'—so much for the prevailing consensus discerned by revisionist historians!—and confirms Cromwell's 'undue optimism that MPs would share his goals and aspirations and that God's will would prevail'. Something of a curate's egg, then, these parliaments.

Security within a search for a settlement is a main theme of Derek Massarella's survey of 'the politics of the army'—that New Model Army gradually growing older—from the complexities of its making at the beginning of 1645, in circumstances which, he points out, have been as much a source of controversy since then as they were at the time. Did formation of a New Model in itself make for a decisive break? Well, victory at Naseby in the event did lead to the collapse of the military arm of the royal cause and, as the pursuit of settlement by other means than war proved difficult, to its own politicisation, radical or otherwise. 1647 was the critical year, when parliament tried to control the monster it had created by sending off some troops to would-be independent Ireland—the British dimension always close by—and by disbanding most of the rest. All this brought itching professional grievances—arrears of pay, indemnity—into the social and political arena at a time when demands for reform were being formulated by the civilian Levellers. Never quite an entity, as Massarella shows throughout, the army, with rank-and-file and junior officer aspirations not consistently in phase with those of the grandees, the army was henceforth a force or perhaps a congeries of forces in politics, almost indeed a fourth estate. Its peculiar contribution to specific situations, e.g. the captivity of the King, and its response to others, kept it in the forefront, helping or impeding the efforts of successive regimes for normalisation in state and society during the 1650s, and even beyond, since the Restoration would not see the total extirpation of a standing army.

The trends of opinion in the army—now left, right, centre, now all three—are traced with perceptiveness by Massarella through the Putney Debates, which have since assumed far more significance than anyone could have guessed at the time, and the second civil war, until Charles's inept divide-and-rule tactics made him his own executioner, handing the axe to a revolutionary force not ashamed to use it, though its leaders were anxious not to appear as a military dictatorship. The new Commonwealth, however, needed an army, not just in England but throughout the usurped Stuart inheritance. The conquests of Ireland and Scotland and the retention of occupying forces in both ensured that the army continued in politics. Yet it was also geographically dispersed, thereby dissipating its sense of unity and in the long run allowing George Monck 'and his boys'—brainwashed and politically neutered—ultimately to bring in Charles Stuart. All through the decade before that the fact of military power affected public perceptions and none more than those of its Commander-in-Chief. Though there was no open military resistance to the establishment of the Protectorate, there was continuous opposition to its continuance, though that was held in check, partly because there was 'an unchangeable belief among [many] army members that Cromwell would not use his considerable power as Lord Protector to advance his own ends', while he for his part recognised that as he made his moves toward settlement he could not afford to jeopardise his own military power base. He would abandon the major-generals and get away with it, but when it came to the offer of the crown he had to hold back, though by doing so he underlined the fact that the army was as much (if not more) an obstacle to 'healing and settling' as a promoter of it. Oliver's death and Richard's resignation made that reality even more apparent. 'The chaos of 1659' was the effect of tension within the army as well as of a discordant body politic. Hence 1660. It is a fascinating story, narrated (in a revised version) here, bringing out the fact that lack of a true—that is single—Good Old Cause in the army robbed it of an ability, time and again, to identify what it really wanted. It lacked, indeed, both the vision and the will to cast one kingdom—the royal term survived even in the speeches of the Lord Protector—let alone three into another mould.

The editor and his contributors are united in the belief that the Interregnum—a period which intermingled pre-war generations and post-Restoration ones—should command attention in its own right for its aspirations and achievements, positive and negative, making it a veritable peak in Hobbes's 'highest of time'. 'Into Another Mould' touches on some of these, but also points to others apt for the attention of historians, in the hope of stimulating an urge among them for further investigation.

Notes

1. Sean Kelsey, *Inventing a Republic: The Political Culture of the English Commonwealth, 1649–1653* (Manchester, 1997).
2. See especially Brendan Bradshaw and John Morrill (eds), *The British Problem c. 1534–1707: State Formation in the Atlantic Archipelago* (London, 1996).
3. Gwyn A. Williams, *When was Wales?* (London, 1985).
4. Ivan Roots, 'Swordsman and Decimators' in R.H. Parry, *The English Civil War and After, 1642–1658* (London, 1970), pp. 78–92.

5. O. Ogle, W.H. Bliss and W.D. McCray, *Calendar of Clarendon State Papers*, 3 vols (Oxford, 1869–76), vol. II, p. 200.
6. J. T. Rutt (ed.), *The Diary of Thomas Burton*, 4 vols (1829); new enlarged edition, ed. Ivan Roots, 4 vols (New York, 1974).
7. 'Oliver Cromwell and his Parliaments' in H.R. Trevor-Roper, *Religion, the Reformation and Social Change* (London, 1967); reprinted in Ivan Roots (ed.), *Oliver Cromwell: A Profile* (London, 1976).

Introduction to the Original Edition published in 1981

Ivan Roots

'If in time, as in place, there were degrees of high and low, I verily believe that the highest of time would be that which passed between the years 1640 and 1660.'[1] These are the opening words of *Behemoth*, Thomas Hobbes's 'history' of the Long Parliament, written but not published in 1668, when he was eighty though, apart from Parkinson's disease, still very much hale in mind and body. His remark is sometimes taken to signify a sort of approval of what happened in those two headlong decades. Nothing could be further from the truth. He goes on—and there is no doubt that in the dialogue of which it forms a part Thomas is talking to Hobbes—

> For he that thence, as from the Devil's Mountain, should have looked upon the world and observed the actions of men, especially in England, might have had a prospect of all kinds of injustice, and of all kinds of folly, that the world could afford . . .[2]

Other men who had felt their world wobble on its axis might well look back less in anger than with nostalgia, but for this political philosopher the only virtue of the upheaval was that the happenings had vindicated his doctrine of sovereignty. (He does not reflect that perhaps without the civil wars and their aftermath he might not have clinched his masterpiece, *Leviathan*.[3]) For him it was a pity that the wickedness and foolishness of those who, notably in the Long Parliament but much elsewhere, had dabbled in social, religious and political sedition, should have worked to the discomfort and worse of so many simple, less powerful, more amenable men. Even so, the notion of 'the highest time' is worth pursuing in the historian's quest for the true inwardness of these years. Whatever that may have been, the events themselves sprawled monstrously across the middle of the seventeenth century, decades which could never be forgotten, desirable though it might be for many to minimise them. Like America, another brave new world, the Interregnum, Restoration or no, could never be undiscovered again. In crisis once more in 1688–9, men remembered 'the late troubles',[4] for encouragement or more often, and in the end more decisively, for warnings.

The catastrophe of 1640–60 had causes. Historians, always hot for origins, have ever since Clarendon and Hobbes spent a great deal of time and ingenuity on causes. Some find them, as James Harrington did in the 1650s,[5] going at least as far back as the early Tudors; others, like Professor G. R. Elton and some of the quickly established early-Stuart revisionist school, seem to find all the combustible material only in the few months preceding the outbreak of civil war in 1642.[6] (But was the Civil War the Revolution itself?) We should not be surprised to learn some day that there was not a civil war at all. Reductionist and a rash of other interpretations have contributed to our understanding—'King Charles and the conspirators', the Puritan Revolution, a bourgeois revolution, a conservative reaction against would-be absolutism or mere incompetence, Court *versus* Country, a general crisis, decentralisation *v.* centralisation, witch-hunters *v.* sceptics, alienated intellectuals, improving landlords, rising, falling, see-sawing gentry, a declining aristocracy, Providence, 'fate, chance, kings and desperate men', besides deep-seated (they are always deep-seated) social and economic forces—all these have been identified and called in to explain or explain away what happened.[7] All are in one way or another inadequate, are errors indeed, but some have been fertile of truth, and present-day historians, even *aficionados* of 'the new history' set off by the social sciences, can, while remaining genuinely puzzled, draw upon all or any of them to come up with hypotheses that may yet fuse into a fully explanatory compound. Even so, we should heed the reminder of Professor Lawrence Stone—he was referring to 'Court *v.* Country' but it applies to any other 'portmanteau' hypothesis—that if by adopting all or any of them 'it is possible powerfully to illuminate many things which were hitherto obscure, [we can do that], only at the expense of obscuring many others'.[8]

But the historical enquiry should not stop short at causes. The course and consequences of the Interregnum now have a greater appeal. This change of emphasis has encouraged Drs Stephen Roberts and Derek Massarella, contributors to this volume, in their research to look, more closely than they might have done twenty years ago, at the 1650s, no longer a neglected decade to be rushed through to usher in the inevitable (if you approve) or sadly unavoidable (if you do not) Restoration of Charles II. There was more to the 1650s than that, as G. E. Aylmer's *The State's Servants*, Christopher Hill's *God's Englishman* and *Milton and the English Revolution*, T. D. Barnard's *Cromwellian Ireland*, F. D. Dow's *Cromwellian Scotland* and many of the essays in Aylmer's *The Interregnum* and the Christopher Hill *festschrift* show.[9] The interest in 'course' now extends beyond 1660 and the assumption that the Restoration somehow broke the back of the century or that it was a watershed, crossroads, turning-point, full-stop, fresh start or whatever comes under review. The theme is not only change but continuity, too, and both must be followed through into the 1660s, 1670s and beyond. It must not be forgotten that if some of the men of 1641 were men of '29, '21 or even '01, many of the men of '79 and '89 were men of '41, '49 and '59. All of these dates have some significance.

Some Intellectual Consequences, Christopher Hill's most recent book,[10] takes up briefly but with a wider range than ever before the problem of the results of what he persists in calling 'the English Revolution' disturbing the earth's diurnal course. It is a firework display—of rockets and damp squibs alike. Can all this, one wonders, be the results of a single revolution, let alone a mere interregnum? Probably not, but all that is offered (*pace* impatient reviewers) is worth some thought. Always be careful with fireworks— damp squibs can go off in your face. Another recent book, less pyrotechnic, *The Stuart Age* by Barry Coward,[11] surveying 1603–1714, may be commended for seeing the century whole, refusing to pause for long at 1660 or even 1689, going so far as to suggest that the Middle Ages came to an end in Robert Walpole, with George I or George II, not Henry VII or Henry VIII, as the last medieval, first modern king.

All this may well demote the Interregnum, to bring us down from Hobbes's 'highest of time'. But it has not yet done so. Instead it argues for continuing investigation of the 1640s and 1650s, both within themselves and in a long perspective which can take in, for instance, Conrad Russell's and others' new views of early Stuart parliaments, not all of which see eye to eye, and the reconsiderations in process of the restored monarchy, and of the glorious, the financial, the commercial revolutions of the late seventeenth and early eighteenth centuries. This present volume may seem not to contribute much to that second search but its authors are aware of the need and do, they believe, offer a few suggestions that might be pursued in a later volume of the 'Exeter Studies in History'. The problems and possibilities of local government, like many of its personnel, overlapped 1660 and went on, both changed and continuous. The army that stood unshiftable and like some watchful estate in the realm throughout the 1650s was at last and with astonishing speed got rid of, most of it, though not all, at the Restoration, but there was always a military dimension, however fluctuating, to government and society from then on. In the last decades of the seventeenth century no longer was there a union, formal or otherwise, of England, Ireland and Scotland, but the history of the peoples of 'these nations', as Cromwell addressed them, had been more inextricably bound together than ever before by the events and tendencies of the Interregnum. Constitutional arrangements since, reflecting or, more characteristically, distorting political, social, economic and cultural relations, weak or strong, have continued to teeter, but if there were any genuine long-term consequences of the Great Rebellion or of the Revolution, the ways in which the constituents of the British Isles have seen themselves and each other are surely a necessary part of them. The moulds made then have been broken and thrown away but something of the shape into which Oliver—and other men from all three countries—crammed them can still be discerned.

Notes

1. T. Hobbes, *Behemoth, or The Long Parliament*, ed. F. Tonnies, 2nd edn, Introduction by M. M. Goldsmith (London, 1969), p. 1.
2. Ibid., p. 1.
3. Whatever else it was, *Leviathan* (1651) was a contribution to the arguments over the Engagement under the Commonwealth. See Q. Skinner, 'Conquest and Consent: Thomas Hobbes and the Engagement Controversy' in G. E. Aylmer (ed.), *The Interregnum* (London, 1972), pp. 79–98.
4. See, for example, the debates in the Convention Parliament of 1689, in which

survivors of the Interregnum like John Birch and Sir John Maynard drew upon their long memories, W. Cobbett (ed.), *Parliamentary History of England*, 36 vols (1806–20), Vol. v.

5. J. Harrington, *Oceana* (1656). Best edition in J. G. A. Pocock (ed.), *The Political Works of James Harrington* (Cambridge, 1977), pp. 155–359. See also R. G. *A Copy of a Letter from an Officer of the Army in Ireland* (1656; reprint, Exeter, 1974).

6. G. R. Elton, *Studies in Tudor and Stuart Politics and Government*, 2 vols (Cambridge, 1974); C. Russell, 'Parliamentary History in Perspective 1604–1629', *History*, 61 (1976), pp. 1–27; C. Russell, *Parliaments and English Politics 1621–1629* (Oxford, 1979); K. Sharpe (ed.), *Faction and Parliament* (Oxford, 1978).

7. The bibliography of this only selective list of interpretations is too vast to set out here. A useful starting point is R. C. Richardson, *The Debate on the English Revolution* (London, 1976).

8. L. Stone, *The Past and the Present* (London, 1981), p. 188.

9. D. H. Pennington and K. Thomas (eds), *Puritans and Revolutionaries: Essays in Seventeenth-Century History presented to Christopher Hill* (Oxford, 1978).

10. C. Hill, *Some Intellectual Consequences ot the English Revolution* (London, 1980).

11. B. Coward, *The Stuart Age* (London, 1981).

1

Union and Disunion in the British Isles, 1637–1660

Ivan Roots

Approaches to the Interregnum

The events of the mid-seventeenth century may be approached in many ways. The usual measure is an English yard laid alongside developments in English national institutions or groups—the monarchy, the Church, Parliament, the Privy Council, the law courts, the peerage, the gentry. Everything comes to a focus in London—Westminster or Whitehall —thence radiating outwards. Another measure much used in the last two or three decades attempts a local dimension, particularly of county communities, each disturbed by internal as well as external tensions. So we find not only the civil war *in* Staffordshire but the civil war *of* Staffordshire, an intense struggle that might well be more absorbing there than the larger conflict. Doubt has recently been cast on the notion of a county community,[1] but quite apart from that historians have noted a role for other topographical units—regions (the far north, the forests), hundreds, cities, even villages—and for other sorts of communities, or particular interests such as trading companies, sects, professions.[2] A man making up his heart and mind to become, say, a royalist, might draw upon his membership of or association with a whole congeries of communities—topographical, professional, kinship, religious. The interactions, contradictions and ambivalences in an individual's or a group's assessment of where their own interests lay helps to explain why in the civil wars the protagonists made shifting coalitions, hot for certainties but prone to get dusty answers. While some historians have scrabbled among the grass roots, others have taken a broader view, relating developments in England to others in Europe. Here is the notion of a general crisis made up of the Frondes, the revolts of the Catalans and of Portugal and so on, in which what was common—or can be made to seem so—was as important, if not more so, than what was peculiar to each of these strikingly contemporaneous conflagrations.[3] The nature of these and of the crisis of which they were apparently symptons are matters of continuing—though lately rather weakening—dispute, which has certainly shed some light, as well as dissipating a great deal of heat.

Somewhere among the grass roots, the national and the general European approaches there may be another avenue worth pursuing. Andrew Marvell's *An Horatian Ode on Cromwell's Return from Ireland* tells us how 'by industrious valour' Oliver Cromwell managed 'to ruin the great work of time' and to 'cast the kingdoms old Into another mould'.[4] What is suggested here is that whatever else happened in the 1640s and 1650s there were striking changes in the relationships of the major constituents of the British Isles: England (with Wales), Scotland and Ireland. What we are looking at is in fact not the *English* Revolution, the *English* Civil Wars, the late troubles in *England*, but a series of interlocking perturbations amounting to a *British* Revolution—if, indeed, there *was* a revolution. If we think of 'troubles' to the point of violence it is clear at once that they did not begin in England. Not until the spring of 1642 did some of the English start with great reluctance seriously to contemplate taking up arms against one another and it was late summer before the first shots were fired in anger. Already by then Scots Covenanters and Irish Catholics were up in rebellions (1638 and 1641 respectively) which were in themselves major influences in bringing the English into civil war. It is, indeed, impossible to understand the 1640s and 1650s without taking into account not only God's Englishmen but also his Scots, Irish and Welshmen, too. This means looking into each constituent in its own right, but also from each to its relations not merely with England but with the others. It was a long period of slow, slow, quick, quick, slow changes throughout the whole British Isles, few isolated, most in some way, not always obvious but usually essentially, connected with each other. The notion of a general crisis of the British Isles might seem more realistic perhaps than one of Europe.

Themes for this crisis include unity and disunity, each of which is relevant to complex situations, full of shifts and ambiguities. The various 'nations'—as Cromwell called them in speeches during which, characteristically, he also lumped them all, Welsh, Scots and Irish, together as English—were in many matters drawn together even as in others they were drifting, even pulling, apart. Something that could keep them together was geography. John of Gaunt's moat, the sea, was defensive not merely to England but Magna Britannia and Hibernia too.[5] The narrowest distance between these two islands, from Fairhead in Antrim to the Mull of Kintyre, is only twelve miles, rather less than the short Channel crossing from Dover to Calais. Between Scotland and England and, of course, between England and Wales, there were only land frontiers, hard to defend, easily and often crossed. The effects of the geographical disposition of the kingdoms were diverse. On the one hand it made for closeness of contacts, much coming and going, trade, migration, cultural and linguistic exchange. On the other it encouraged friction, competition, misunderstandings, border-raids, even invasion with hopes of conquest. Sometimes it is easier to appreciate people distant, rarely seen, than those nearer, on the spot as it were. The quarrels of political neighbours are like domestic squabbles, often fierce, even murderous, though ironically, soonest patched up—until next time, anyway. What can be felt in the mid-seventeenth century—and can be still glimpsed today, when relationships within these islands are again in flux—is a mingled urge towards independence and interdependence, and a sense of common interest shading into hostility.

Scotland before the Covenant

First, Scotland. Bishop Burnet's remark that 'the late Civil Wars' had their 'first beginning' there is often quoted, but not always in full. He goes on: 'there can be no clear understanding of what followed until these first disorders there be truly stated'.[6] The historian, then, even the one with an exclusively English concern, must keep at least half an eye upon Scotland. Whatever happened in England was preceded by and went along—not always in parallel, nor in the same plane, nor even at the same pace—with developments in Scotland. The two kingdoms were already in 1637 ravelled up together. The Scottish National Covenant was certainly an expression of a distinct Scottish nationalism, a call for breaking a real or imaginary dependence upon England and thus in some sort anti-English, proclaiming a refusal to be dragged along on the coat-tails of a richer, more populous neighbour with social, cultural, economic traits and interests different from, even somewhat inimical to, the Scots'. But that is not the only story that can or should be made of the Covenant. Look back to the mid-sixteenth century. The English Reformation had been mostly led by the Tudor Crown—the Scottish one, which had come later, was driven against the Stuarts' indignation. The English, a stiff-necked confident people, stressed their long traditions of being an elect nation—to the point of claiming that God is English.[7] The Scots' religious experience was different. John Knox and his associates felt they could appeal only to a more recent intervention by God and so elucidated the immediate intentions of Providence in a specific gesture, one making Scotland a covenanted nation. But they thought that the ultimate impact must surely be the same both sides of the border. God expected both his old English and his new Scots to embrace one true religion and to establish that by a common effort, a British effort. God then, was British, or would be if men would let him. Speaking English and encouraging that tongue in Scotland, Knox and company saw themselves not as strangers to England, 'but in a manner your own countrymen, so the Isle [i.e. Great Britain] is a common country to us both . . . one of the same religon'. Some were optimistic enough to extend that aspiration to Ireland: imagining 'a reformed Ireland . . . brought to a perfection of obedience . . .'. The British Isles would then have become a 'certain monarchy in itself and in the ocean divided from the rest of the world'. (The sea again, seen as a barrier externally, but also an internal binding force.)[8]

So a Scottish national consciousness, inextricably associated with the Kirk, the most valuable thing on earth, argued for a more, not a less, intimate relationship—even a 'brotherhood'—with England. Similar church discipline and doctrine in England would guarantee their survival in Scotland. Supporters in the National Covenant went so far as to refer to 'the greatest blessing that God has bestowed on this isle . . . next the Christian faith, was the union of the two kingdoms under one head', that of James VI and I.[9] It was a sentiment not much shared in England. James told the English that they had gained from union with Wales—'and is not Scotland greater than Wales?'. That, of course, was the rub. Wales was too small to threaten any aspect of English life. Scotland had a larger population, a greedy untamed nobility, a long tradition of anti-English alliance with foreign powers. A firmer union seemed a threat and James's identification of himself in 1604 as 'the husband and the whole isle is my lawful wife' was unappealing.[10] James himself went on to concentrate his attention on England, governing Scotland by proxy with his pen.[11] Under his successor, the Stuart monarchy became even more remote from its origins. Sharing the commonsense drive of European rulers with diversified territories to bring them into some kind of uniformity, Charles I ruled from London, robbing his northern kingdom of the presence of a royal court, the rewards of patronage and whatever, reminding Scots of Henry VII's prediction of the likely fruits of the marriage of his daughter Margaret to James IV—a union that was 'an accession not of England to Scotland, but of Scotland to England'.[12] The distrust already aroused by James VI's Articles of Perth was increased by his son's own Act of Revocation and the assignment to the bishops of a direct, indeed a conspicuous role in secular as well as in spiritual affairs. His behaviour during his visit in 1633 for his coronation, the ritual then, the consequent canons of uniformity and finally the new prayer book raised the cry of 'the Kirk in danger!'. The upshot was the Covenant of 1638, which looked as if it were both anti-monarchical and anti-English and was neither.[13]

Scotland from the Covenant to the Engagement

The Covenant was, in fact, directed against the King's evil counsellors, who were more Scots than English, and against religious innovations (chiefly associated with William Laud) which were known to be unacceptable also to many in England. Covanters were aware, too, of political and social strains and disappointments in England not unlike their own. For example, Laud's stepping up of tithes paralleled the Revocation. Immediate contacts with English Puritans hinted at a possible common cause of religion,[14] liberties, laws and estates. The chauvinism of the Covenant did not preclude a recognition that if Charles I of Scotland was being misled, so was Charles I of England. Hence some Scots were not displeased that their 'business' brought on, first the Short, and then the Long Parliament, since it was certain that the King would not be incontinently provided by them with the wherewithal to bring the rebels to heel. The presence of a Scottish army in the north of England and the treaty of Ripon ensured that for his part Charles could not easily dispense with a parliament bent on redress of grievances which included the elimination of Laud and Strafford, men as unfit for the state of Scotland as for that of England. Charles's clear recognition of links between his critics in both kingdoms was underlined by his northern journey in the summer of 1641 when he set out to separate them by offering concessions in Scotland. The Additional Instruction was John Pym's answer to the King's patent tactics there,[15] and in the event all Charles succeeded in doing was to heighten the political temperature within each kingdom rather than to incite animosities between them.

Then came the Ulster rebellion of October 1641, which directly affected Scots as well as English interests, and brought the core of opposition in each country, if anything, even tighter together. Once civil war broke out in England, Pym exploited the situation by working for a Solemn League and Covenant between the two countries. Attained before he died in 1643, this was one of his many contributions to parliament's ultimate victory, though not as major as it was first thought it would be. What the English wanted was a civil league and the Scottish army that would go with it. For the Scots it was the Covenant that appealed most, making explicit what was implied in 1638 that both nations must work together in the sight of God to preserve the Kirk by extending the one reformed and true religion into England. Hence the bitterness of that inflexible Covenanter Robert Baillie about the failure of the Assembly of Divines at Westminster to come up with anything more than 'a lame Erastian presbytery'. That was not just an immediate blow at Scotland but a betrayal of traditional hopes of a dedicated British nation of Scots and English confidently striding together, elect and covenanted, 'bosom brethren, one flesh and blood'.[16] Some Covenanters had even talked of taking an elated British army into the Continent to spread the really reformed religion there, while in Ireland another jointly would reduce the rebels, spreading Presbyterianism, praising God and at the same time securing Scotland and England.

The Scots, in fact, wanted religious unity to the point of obsession, pursuing 'one union of this island, one form of Kirks, one confession of faith, one catechism, one directory for the worship of God'.[17] That spiritual aim, they recognised, called for civil union, too. So they accepted a Committee of Both Kingdoms. So did the English parliament, but its motivation was only secondarily religious. The Scottish army seemed essential in the dark days when it was first called in. Certainly its presence in the north of England tied down royalist forces there, but as the English parliamentary armies gradually advanced towards superiority, there were reports that some 'did leap for joy' at Scottish failures. Even Presbyterians were inclined to see union as an invitation to Scots, who though Presbyterian were still Scots, to interfere in English affairs, giving them an 'unwelcome power over us'. The growth of Independency and the proliferation of sects meant even more resentment of Scottish rigidity, while intensifying strains between army and parliament which would eventually become political. Similarly, in Scotland itself Montrose's victories, won in part with Irish catholic forces, made Scottish domestic politics more complicated.[18] So between 1646 and 1649 both kingdoms were in continuous tension, if not revolution, even if, as English revisionist historians are rushing to point out, there was also consensus on many points of parliamentary politics.

Charles's surrender to the Scots reflected his considered judgement that it would not be hard to break up the uneasy political alliances forged by his enemies—and so he would be King again. For the Scots to transfer him to parliament was an unwelcome surprise, suggesting that there were still optimists about who could envisage an ultimate union. But the cynical Engagement he negotiated in 1647 shattered residual unity again between the Scots and the English, between the English army and the parliament and in Scotland among the Covenanters themselves. The second civil war testifies to Charles's success in finding means towards his objective, his execution to his failure to reach it.

Scotland in the 1650s and beyond

The Scots were now a fragmented nation undergoing political and even social revolution.[19] Though no party was willing to accept the unilateral English abolition of the national monarchy, not everyone was convinced of sincerity in the readiness of Charles, Prince of Wales, to take the Covenant. It was apparent that he came to Scotland on his way to England and though he promised 'to endeavour a complete union of the kingdoms', each of which had 'an unquestionable and undeniable interest in his person as king of both',[20] many felt that once in London he would follow James VI and Charles I as an absentee. Defeats by Cromwell at Dunbar (1650) and Worcester (1651) were not unwelcome to every patriotic Scot. (Equally if Charles had won many an English royalist would have been unhappy that he should receive his southern kingdom back from alien hands.) As it happened, Cromwell's victories would lead on to a union, but one in a new mould, into which Scotland was poured by an iron hand in an iron glove. There was no question now of the Kirk being imposed upon England, indeed its very existence in Scotland was in jeopardy, given a state religious policy which offered toleration while preventing Presbyterians from patently political preaching. Scotland over the next few years was ruled in English interests, 'as when the poor bird is embodied into the hawk that has eaten it up'.[21] Yet things could have been worse. There was no attempt to make Scotland a colony, thrown open to planters and adventurers, though the Rump set up a Committee (September 1651) to draft a measure declaring 'the right of this Commonwealth to so much of Scotland as is now under [our] forces'. This resulted in a bill 'asserting the right of England to Scotland'. But that brutal claim soon gave way to a more feasible scheme to create 'one commonwealth and free state' out of the two nations.[22] Following discussions with appropriate (i.e. reasonably amenable) Scottish interest groups, 'deputies' came down to London. Worried that the union intended was undefined and carried with it their acceptance of 'we know not what', they were still talking it over when Cromwell expelled the Rump. Barebone's, too, considered union but resigned before anything was settled.

The Instrument of Government assumed a union with Scottish (and Irish) representation in an imperial parliament. Ordinances issued in 1654 under clause xxx of the Instrument provided for a union with Scotland at least and for distribution of parliamentary seats in both countries.[23] But neither contained anything like a Solemn League and Covenant or a Committee of Both Kingdoms. Scotland remained under a military-dominated Council of State and was administratively in essence a subordinate entity, though given a prospect of 'healing and settling' into a more relaxed relationship. However, the first Protectorate Parliament failed to confirm the union and other relevant ordinances. The second parliament accepted the union in the measure of 12 April 1657 which confirmed a mass of ordinances 'in a lump'. So did the Humble Petition and Advice, which had the considerable advantage—or so it was expected—over the Instrument of having a parliamentary sanction.[24] But in the 1659 parliament (Richard Cromwell's) commonwealthsmen, still smarting from the expulsion of 1653, the abrupt dissolution of February 1658, and frustrated by their inability in spite of their mastery of procedure to prevent formal recognition of 'the Single Person', insisted on assailing to the point of 'great noise and horrid confusion' the presence in their midst of 'Scottish members' who were seen both as elements alien in culture and interests and in the pockets of the executive—which some, though perhaps not all, of them certainly were. Burton's *Diary* records a great deal of what was said and it testifies

8

to the stubborn survival of traditional Scotophobia, reinforced by more recent experience, resistant to the argument of 'the Court' that union between England, Ireland and Scotland would become 'a strong treble cord twisted together' that would not be easily broken, unless foolishly it were untwisted. Scotland was sneered at as a province 'at best', its inhabitants 'foreigners' with no colour to be represented at Westminster. If Scots were admitted why not members from Jamaica? On the other hand there were some vigorous defences of union, calling on the long and short-term interests of both Scotland and England. But the main thrust of the debates was towards criticism of the character and very existence of the Protectorate and they are another illustration—a particularly vivid and circumstantial one—of the way in which the interlocking of the three kingdoms had an impact upon the internal politics of each.[25]

Throughout the Protectorate many Englishmen thought they had been particularly generous to the Scots in imposing union. 'What greater favour could they cast upon you?' In his *Memoirs* Edmund Ludlow looked back to 'how great a condescension' it was.[26] For many Scots it was an insult and an injury. The Kirk, denied its General Assembly, saw it as even worse than an obscene travesty of the British union they had envisaged only a decade before. Favouring diversity and controversy in religion, the Cromwellian union spat in the face of a rigid Presbyterianism that still could not think it possible it might be mistaken. But some Scots, more venal or maybe more politic, could glimpse the two countries 'homogeneated by naturalisation and the mutual enjoyment of the same privileges and immunities', even sharing the same burdens. This would produce a real 'Great Britain'. Meanwhile resistance continued in the craggy and papist Highlands, where the English, unenthusiastic even about the more settled Lowlands, deplored a wild people who 'generally speak Irish [*sic*], go only with plads about their middle, both men and women', 'savage beasts', 'bloody-minded', 'base and beggarly', living —wilfully seems to be implied—in houses 'only of earth and turfs'.[27] Union with people like that could hardly be contemplated.

When the Rump was restored in May 1659 it repudiated naturally enough—though perhaps impolitically—all that had been done in its 'exile'. But, significantly on a Scottish initiative, a bill for union was brought in, to be nipped in the bud at the expulsion in August. It is ironical that when the Restoration of 1660 came to England it came in effect from Scotland. George Monck's success in settling North

Britain,[28] ostensibly in the name and interests of the various regimes he had served under in the 1650s, enabled him to march his brain-washed army slowly upon London during the winter of 1659–60, confident that behind him there was an urge for order and stability among Scots, many of whom pressed him to see the union maintained. The Rump, restored yet again, toyed with the notion of an act of union but dissolved itself before it neared completion. The Convention of 1660 did nothing about it and Charles II came back without any commitment to it, or for that matter to the Covenant he had sworn to ten years before. So a separate Scotland, quite unrepresented in either chamber at Westminster, got back its own parliament and its own administration. But both were under heavy pressure from English court-politicians and the country was greatly discriminated against economically and socially. The reign of Charles II was a black period which made the 1650s seem like a golden age. For his own reasons Charles II was not inimical to negotiations for a union in 1668–9. Scottish commissioners once again made the long trek to London. Discussions echoed the phraseology of the past: 'two kingdoms . . . united into one monarchy . . . inseparably and . . . the name of that monarchy shall be Great Britain'.[29] The scheme foundered largely because of Scottish disappointment at the small amount of representation adjudged sufficient for them and because of English coolness to the whole 'package'. When the Revolution of 1688–9 raised the spectre of a separate Scottish monarchy in the old Stuart line, a few concessions were given to them by the new one under William III. But it was not until the Hanoverian succession was in clear prospect under Anne, that the matter was seriously canvassed again 'as necessary not for any actual good it could possibly do but to avoid a probable evil'.[30] The crisis was resolved by a union painfully formed in 1707, one in which Scotland lost her parliament, but retained some of her national institutions like the Kirk and the legal system. It seemed to be—was certainly so put over—in the interests of significant groups in both countries. Though it was assailed fiercely from the start it has somehow survived to come under heavy fire in recent years when relationships within the British Isles seem to skirt again the brink of crisis, with many Scots preferring 'a poor independent sovereignty' for Scotland to 'a small share in a great one'.[31]

Ireland before the Ulster Rebellion

If seventeenth-century English attitudes towards the Scots were born of ignorance strengthened by prejudice, so, too, were those they adopted towards the Irish—and they were even more intolerant. Politically England and Ireland had had contacts older and more intimate than those between independent Scotland and England. The connection went back to the reign of Henry II in the twelfth century when barons like Richard Strongbow, Earl of Pembroke, realised the possibilities of carving out territories and the political power that went with them over there. The aim became one of reducing the bulk of the native Irish to helots. Wave after wave of immigrants, not large in number maybe but vigorous and greedy, imposed a range of would-be elites who became collectively 'the Old English' neo-Irish. By conquest and confiscation they acquired the land before they became the land's. But gradually they did develop interests and ways of life which were not those of the mother-land, where the attention of the government was all too often distracted from Ireland by internal problems, like the Wars of the Roses, or by policies pursued elsewhere, notably towards France and Scotland. But the English crown never completely gave up a direct concern for what went on in Dublin and beyond. Ireland was well on the way to being an English colony long before Elizabethan expeditions were sent to North America. The expanding and contracting Pale around Dublin, where, for centuries, only English power was really effective and outside which its authority hardly existed, paralleled the narrow American seaboard beyond which was Indian country. But as in America the foothold was bound sooner or later to turn into a platform for the taking of the whole country. Irish aspirations for independence with or without allegiance to the English crown were always dashed by the fact that England could and did cut their island off from direct continental contacts, especially out of fear that otherwise Ireland might become a base for invasion—as it was for the Pretenders in the reign of Henry VII, who as an invader himself could appreciate the problem. It assumed great importance with the Reformation. Both the native Irish and the Old English clung to Catholicism, each group in its own way associating religion with an incipient nationalism and making it a potent symbol of 'Ireland their own'. In turn Irish popery increased English distrust and encouraged a will to break out of the Pale until the whole island was under control —and paying for it. Ironically the first systematic moves towards plantation (settled colonisation) came under the Catholic rule of Philip and Mary. Queen's and King's counties suggested a pattern of dispossession and seizure that would endure for a century or more. By the middle of the reign of Elizabeth I conquest was the consistent policy and English settlers and the armies that preserved them increasingly took the line that the native Irish in their bogs were 'little better than cannibals that do hunt one another, more uncivil, more unreliant, more barbarous and more brutish in their customs and demeanours than in any part of the world',[32] and that it was therefore 'a civic duty' for 'duty and obedience' to be imposed on them 'by fear and force'. Those whom we intend to exploit we must first make contemptible.

Revolts followed by confiscations and implantations into the seventeenth century determined that relationships with the various strains of the Irish population would remain tense. The union of the crowns of England and Scotland in 1603 was an event equally in Irish history. Scots had, of course, been interested in Ireland over a long period. Common Celtic origins, linguistic and cultural affinities lasting well into the later Middle Ages, and geography—Scotland, remember, is closer to Ireland than either England or Wales is—all argued for impacts upon one another. Under the Bruces conquest itself was attempted as something more than a mere counter to English aspirations there. Thenceforth concern, though fluctuating, never petered out. Under Elizabeth I Scottish penetration of nearby Ulster began and was not resisted by her. The aftermath of the Flight of the Earls in 1607 quickened the process. Not unexpectedly the Scots, whether on royal plantations, as individual adventurers or simply as hopeful tenants on the estates of (often absentee) English landlords, proved to be dour, determined settlers.[33] The character of the province of Ulster was largely fixed by them. It survives to this day—the Rev. Ian Paisley refers to himself as an Ulster Scot. The religious complexion of Ireland now included Presbyterianism, lay and clerical, for the Scots took ministers with them. This ran up against the 'Anglican' policy for the Church of Ireland pursued by Lord Deputy Thomas Wentworth, inspired by Laud. When Scotland rose in 1638 Wentworth was quick, too quick in fact, to sense a likely collusion between Ulster Scots and Covenanters and to see them using the province as 'a back door' into England. He resisted Hamilton's scheme to colonise Derry where the City of London was dawdling, even though like himself Hamilton was a king's man. He sought to impose 'a black oath' whereby Scots in Ireland were formally to express repudiation of the

Covenant. Yet Ulster was not socially, politically nor even religiously a mirror-image of noble-dominated Kirk-ridden Lowland Scotland and Wentworth clumsily excited avoidable animosities.[34] More to his point would have been an alliance of Ulster Scots with the newer Protestant English settlers in the implementation of his aim of converting fragmented Ireland into a single polity contributing to the interests of the Anglo-Scottish monarchy with which he identified his own. It meant creating an Ireland as uniform as he wanted England itself to become. Instead he made himself more and more isolated and when he was called back home to cope, too late, with 'the Scottish business', his system such as it was collapsed.

Ireland during the 1640s

The Long Parliament met under the shadow of a possible coup from Strafford (as he now was) based on the intervention of a disciplined, largely papist Irish army. 'You have an army in Ireland you may use to reduce this kingdom'—he could have meant England or Scotland or both. Certainly both Covenanters and the English parliamentary majority looked askance at Ireland, with the former anxious to keep their forces on foot in all three kingdoms and the latter to get rid of Strafford, to keep an eye on the unreliable royal army in the north of England and to prevent the King from coming to terms with the Scots there. When rebellion was raised by the native Irish—papists to a man—the Scots were quick to send forces there to protect their own interests. Curiously enough, though it was said the Irish hated the Scots perfectly, in the very early stages of the rising they left them alone, no doubt in the hope of separating them from the English.[35] If that was so, the gambit failed and soon English and Scots were a single enemy. The rebellion, which dramatically intensified English domestic politics, was also formative in Scottish internal affairs. By the end of 1641 the crisis was already one sucking in three kingdoms at odds with each other and within themselves. It needed only the outbreak of actual fighting in England to engulf the whole British Isles.

Very quickly the Old English were in alliance with the native rebels, under a confederate banner proclaiming support for 'one God, one King, one Country'. (The King was conveniently misled by evil advisers, a misfortune to which kings in all ages have been prone.) Though Charles said at once that suppression was 'his chief business', he was in fact very dilatory about it, giving a priority to seeking political, soon to become military, support for action at home. Pym and his associates were unwilling to trust him with a military wherewithal that might be turned inward upon themselves.[36] The Grand Remonstrance, with which they consciously risked breaking the uneasy parliamentary front, raised *inter alia* the whole question of military power in England—and perhaps, even as early, that of sovereignty, too—and led on to the Militia Ordinance, the Commissions of Array, the Nineteen Propositions and the King's Answer, paper skirmishes, postures of defence, and at length military standards raised. Civil war, which was the least expected outcome of the collapse of the Personal Government in 1640, had come by August 1642 to England (and Wales), Scotland and Ireland. There were armies everywhere, covenanted, confederated, associated and whatever. The military—and it followed political—consequences of all this were incalculable.

Though both King and parliament concentrated on developments within England and Wales, they could never quite forget Ireland. Each intended sooner or later to reduce and punish the insubordinate colony. Charles, however, could see an immediate advantage towards his English objectives in coming to some arrangement with rebels who claimed, like parliament, to fight actually on his behalf, to extricate him· from evil advisers, Jesuits on the one interpretation, Protestants on the other. An Irish truce would release for intervention in England and Wales his own forces presently bogged down over there and perhaps even allow the recruitment of some rebel troops into his armies. Charles might argue that since it was clearly in the interests of the parliamentarians 'to improve and continue the rebellion',[37] a negotiated break in the Irish struggle was not only necessary for his own preservation but for that of his loyal subjects in both kingdoms. Hence he entered without shame into 'the Cessation' of 1643. 'Politically disastrous' it certainly was, alienating parliament further and dividing the royalists. It was hard to counter the propaganda charge that the King was inveterately 'soft' on popery. But initially at least it did give him some military gains, more, it has been suggested, than has been commonly supposed.[38] Troops from Ireland stiffened the royalist effort in North Wales and its borders—and Wales was, after all, a 'chief nursery' of his armies. This accretion of strength may well have made the war in England last longer, while in Scotland Montrose's spectacular advances could have owed something to Irish levies, distracting such attention as the Covenanters were able to give to their supporting role to parliament in northern England. Since many Scots shared the English estimate of the 'cruel savagery' of the Irish, the Cessation inflamed opinion there, too.

The Cessation did not in fact mean complete and unbroken peace in Ireland. The Scots army in Ulster, supplied and encouraged from the Lowlands, fought on and as soon as Charles's defeat in England was certain it was politically desirable for parliament to contemplate an early campaign throughout Ireland. The 'Presbyterian' parliamentary majority regarded the New Model as 'a mere mercenary army' at their behest.[39] Why not send some of its regiments over there, where they would be decently distanced from English politics—consensus or otherwise—and kept busy about useful tasks assigned to them by their civilian masters? Who pays the piper calls the tune, but only so long as he pays up. Already by early 1647 army pay was in arrears, the soldiers' professional grievances were palpable and their redress could easily become a political aspiration. The regiments nominated refused to go and before long the army was an estate in the realm. Thus Ireland like Scotland remained a living issue in English political developments. 'The search for a settlement' which has been fairly taken to characterise the next few years was not just an English but an emphatically British requirement.

The execution of the King, formative as we have seen in both Scottish internal politics and Anglo-Scotch relations, marked a stage also for Ireland. The Rump was determined to break the Cessation, to crush the long festering rebellion there and to make the Irish pay financially and otherwise for the nuisance they had been now for nearly a decade. Moreover, security demanded denial of the island to royalists in exile and to their potential foreign allies, who now included those Scots who wre hankering after their House of Stuart. Ireland once conquered, the confiscations intended since 1642 could be effected, with some at least of the proceeds diverted to reduce the English armies' dangerous arrears. So Cromwell was sent as the instrument of that Providence in whom he trusted, though characteristically he extracted from the Rump cash enough to pay his troops for a brisk campaign, being as aware as Strafford had been that money is as much the sinews of military discipline as it is of civil government. Even so, his preparations coincided with the last real fling of regimental radicalism in mutinies at Northampton and Burford, somewhat reminiscent of the 1647 resistance to drafting to Ireland. As it was, the suppression of the army Levellers augured well for a swift effective campaign. The story of Cromwell in Ireland is well known. Of its military impact there is no doubt. The terror that was part of it and its significance in our estimate of Cromwell's character and achievement remain matters of living controversy. What can be said is that his actions were in line with some contemporary views of legitimate military tactics and were resonant with 'respectable' English attitudes towards the Irish. Marvell's *Horatian Ode*, with all its ambiguities about Cromwell and his English ambitions, sees no occasion for a moral judgement upon this particular episode.[40]

Cromwellian Ireland

Within months most of Ireland was reduced. Though it was the Lord's work, Cromwell himself clearly regarded the campaign as a distraction from his ultimate ambitions, which lay elsewhere. He soon returned home leaving his adroit son-in-law, Henry Ireton, to complete the conquest. Ireton was dead within a couple of years—an event not without significance for England as well as Ireland—and it took several more years within a *de facto* union to effect anything like a settlement. Cromwell himself, even as Lord Protector of the three kingdoms, seemed only fitfully interested and if we are to speak of Cromwellian Ireland it is either in a very loose sense or with specific reference not so much to Oliver as to Henry Cromwell, who, overlapping and then following the insipid Charles Fleetwood as Lord Deputy, moulded policy there from 1655 to 1659. The effort could have been one merely of conquest, of unmitigated punishment and revenge, making 'a wilderness and calling it peace'. Many in England and Scotland would have approved of that. In fact what was done was of some complexity, with developments going in different directions at different paces, responding in part to political tergiversations back home and in part to the diverse attitudes of the administrators on the spot, chiefly military, some of them like Edmund Ludlow quite hostile to the very existence of the Protectorate.[41] In part, too, the process of change and continuity was affected by the actions and reactions of various Irish interest and pressure groups, from the natives (not much) to the new adventurers and the holders of debentures on confiscated land. (Many of these were rank-and-file soldiers who disposed of them for quick money to speculators, mostly their own officers—a power bloc which would in some measure survive the Restoration.) Once again Scotland cannot be left out of the tally. Conflicts there betwen Resolutioners (ready to accept Charles II) and

Remonstrants (inveterately inimical to him) spread to Ulster, presenting the administration with such political as well as religious problems that a transplantation of Resolutioners to the south-west was seriously contemplated. Eventually more conciliatory attitudes on both sides eased the situation. In this a prominent part was played by Roger Boyle, Lord Brogill, Lord President of the Scottish Council in the mid-1650s.[42]

Broghill, son of 'the great Earl of Cork', was a leading light among 'the Old Protestants' (the 'new' English and Scots of the Elizabethan and early Stuart plantations). The likely organiser of 'the kinglings' who in the parliament of 1656–58 offered Cromwell the crown, Broghill was a man of three kingdoms, whose policy within and between all three was to create stability by establishing what would be in effect a coalition of moderates and conservatives, drawing in 'the natural rulers' of the kingdoms. For Ireland his means was to get Henry Cromwell, whose sensible 'art-of-the-possible' temperament he quickly discerned, to work for the political ascendancy of the well-landed Old Protestants over the Catholics (whether natives or Old English) on the one hand, and the new Protestants (adventurers or debenture-holders) on the other. In England Oliver Cromwell had to refuse the crown and much of Broghill's programme faltered. In Scotland ultimate authority still lay in the Commander-in-Chief, George Monck, more consistently enigmatic than encouraging. But from 1656 onwards Henry Cromwell did come somewhat more reliably up to expectations.

There was, we know, a land revolution in Ireland during the Interegnum. It has been estimated that in 1640 nearly two-thirds of Ireland was in Catholic (chiefly Old English) hands but by 1660 little more than a fifth remained there.[43] Many of the new owners were, of course, debenture-holders and adventurers and one would have expected the political balance to have tipped towards them. In fact as the 1650s wore on it went to the Protestants previously settled—the Old Protestants, the Broghills as it were. They had to work for it. Many had been royalists in the 1640s, suspected of malignancy for years afterwards by propagandists of the Good Old Cause. Henry Cromwell, beginning to direct policy from 1655 onwards, was more willing to offer 'oblivion', recognising how much stability across the three states which somehow or other had come into the charge of his father (to whom he was devoted) depended upon the co-operation of men with a permanent stake—'a fixed interest', in Ireton's term—in society. As early as 1649 some Old Protestants had shown a willingness to give that co-operation, sensing that since the military regime was clearly powerful enough to stay for at least a while, it would be impolitic, if not self-spiting, to offer blind opposition. If they had articulated their instinctive reactions they would no doubt have used some of the same arguments as those deployed at the same time in England in support of the Engagement of 1650. But their line generally was as practical as that of the Earl of Leicester in taking the Engagement—he wanted to be able to take tenants in arrears to court.[44] The Old Protestants set out to mitigate the policy of 'Hell or Connaught', not because of any squeamishness about the hardship it inflicted upon the natives, but because the exile of 'the meaner sort of people' would rob themselves of the cheap labour force they needed for the proper exploitation of their estates. Recruitment of Protestant field-workers from England and Wales would have helped but was unlikely since settlement in Ireland was even less appealing to 'the inferior sort' than in America. But the Old Protestants had no objection to the transportation of Catholic *proprietors* and the confiscation and re-distribution of their estates, indeed there was little they could see against it. But many military men and some commissioners wanted revenge for the legendary massacres of '41, blood calling out for blood; they would wipe out popery at all levels of society. That urge was strong among the Baptists and some of these were also vigorous opponents of the Protectorate on ideological grounds. Maintaining contacts with critics in England—as did commonwealthsmen, fifth monarchists and sectaries —they were prepared to be obstructive on both sides of the Irish Sea. The army in Ireland can indeed be considered a major centre of opposition to the sort of settlement with 'somewhat of monarchical in it' that Broghill was backing in England and Scotland. Nearer at home the Old Protestants saw in army debenture-holders, more and more of them officers, well-placed political and economic rivals. Unlike the new adventurers, often absentees, some leaving their lands to lie literally waste, debenture-holders were on the spot, many ready to stay and make the most of what they could get hold of. All this encouraged the Old Protestants to look to Henry Cromwell. Kept well-informed by John Thurloe of what was happening in England and Scotland, he was inclined to see them as a counter to the instability inherent in the regime with which he had to cope.

The Henrician settlement in Ireland was watched from and discussed in all three kingdoms. Apart from its general impact, it had a particular influence at a critical time. Under the terms of the Humble Petition and

Advice Oliver Cromwell could nominate his own successor as Protector. On his deathbed he appears to have given his voice to his eldest surviving son, Richard, inexperienced, untried. This decision made for comment at the time and has ever since. Why did he not choose Henry, able, tested, bright? One reason must have been that Henry by his very policies in Ireland had excited in the army in Ireland animosities which had spread to England. He was considered personally ambitious and too open to, if not party to, the manoeuvres of the ex-malignant (and some probably still royalist) Old Protestants, and over-tolerant, too, of Catholics. His moves, somewhat successful, towards stability hinted at a reduction in the need for substantial military forces. The opposition to the sitting of Irish members, which was as fierce as that to the Scots in the debates in Richard's parliament,[45] was perhaps as much against Henry as against the Protectorate itself. This view is reinforced by the speed with which the restored Rump put Henry out of office and set out to rule Ireland more or less direct from Westminster and on very different lines, with heavy taxes to relieve fiscal burdens in England and economic restrictions which would impinge on Old Protestant enterprise. The result was the *de facto* union of England and Ireland which was less acceptable now to the Old Protestants and from then on they worked against it. Broghill might have assured Thurloe in 1659 that they would never set up for themselves, making Ireland 'a back door to let Charles Stuart into England . . . interest as well as duty will keep us from so ruinous a wickedness'.[46] 'Interest cannot lie' said Harrington at about the same time, but men can lie about it and it is likely that Broghill was a royalist well before George Monck revealed himself in the spring of 1660. An Irish convention dominated by Old Protestants met at the same time as the English one to add its weight to those summoning Charles II back, but also, as important, to do what it could to retain and extend the ascendancy they had worked so hard for throughout the 1650s. On the whole they succeeded.

Throughout the seventeenth century, whether under early or later Stuarts or during the Interregnum, Ireland was regarded in England as 'far enough [away] to be treated as a colonisable area, but near enough to be governable by the English state in its own interests rather than be abandoned to the colonists and theirs'.[47] The attitude of the colonists themselves, whether Old Protestants or the newcomers of the 1650s, was ambiguous. They wanted to be left alone, but at the same time they could recognise a need for the support, indeed the protection, of England against internal dissension even if that was not pushed to the point of open rebellion, with or without help from abroad. Memories of men of '41 survived in Ireland even as they survived of different men of '41 in England. What the English Protestant ascendancy, merging with the Scots of Ulster, did not want in 1660 and afterwards was a union, *de facto* or otherwise, that would restrict themselves. They had taken advantage of the Cromwellian regime and intended fully to take advantage of its successors. It is difficult and quite unnecessary to disagree with Dr Toby Barnard's conclusion that the character of the Protestant ascendancy was 'largely formed' in the 1650s and was the Cromwellians' 'enduring contribution to Ireland'.[48] As such it was one of the few identifiable permanent consequences of the Interregnum—and it was one of significance not only for Ireland but for Scotland, England and Wales, indeed the whole British Isles.

Conclusion: the General Crisis of the British Isles

If there is any value in seeking common features in or interactions between coincident events, it is more likely to be found in such intimately related entities as England, Wales, Scotland and Ireland than in the disparate—still in spite of the EU wildly disparate—elements of Western Europe. Englishmen were directly involved in Scotland and Ireland, Scots in England and Ireland, Irishmen (though admittedly in smaller numbers) in England and Scotland, and Welshmen in all of them during the 1640s and 1650s. Few if any of these people were sucked into the Frondes, the Revolt of the Catalans or Cossack risings on the remote steppes of Central Asia. The close relations of the constituents of the British Isles were made by geography, long history and interest. The last of these binding forces was at its tightest perhaps in those excited years between the Covenant of 1637 and the surprising Restoration of 1660, during which some common institutions were set up, if only temporarily—the Committee of Both Kingdoms and those unwillingly imperial parliaments of the Protectorate. This was something more than the union of the crowns of England and Scotland in 1603 and the long-standing claims of the English crown to all of Ireland. The comings and goings between the islands and over the land-frontiers were more frequent than ever before and for a long time afterwards, and the movements were not solely those of men in arms, but of ideas, political, cultural and scientific, not touched upon here but certainly an intrinsic part of the new moulding, which was broken though perhaps not quite shattered with the collapse of the republic.

We are accustomed to thinking of the times going up like parchment in the fire in England during the Interregnum. We should extend the range, imagining, if we must have a revolution, the British rather than the English, visualising the Great British Rebellion, seeing 'the late troubles' as the products of all three kingdoms. Perhaps the best label to put on such complex events and developments, hard enough to interpret even if we confine our attention to England, would be 'The General Crisis of the British Isles'.

Notes

1. G. Holmes, 'The County Community in Stuart Historiography', *Journal of British Studies*, 19 (1980), pp. 54–73.
2. I. Roots, 'Interest—Public, Private and Communal' in R. H. Parry (ed.), *The English Civil War and After, 1642–1658* (London, 1970), pp. 111–21 and *The Late Troubles in England* (Exeter, 1969).
3. See e.g. T. H. Aston (ed.), *Crisis in Europe 1560–1660* (1965) and G. Parker and L. M. Smith (eds), *The General Crisis of the Seventeenth Century* (1978).
4. E. S. Donno (ed.), *Andrew Marvell: The Complete Poems* (Harmondsworth, 1972), pp. 55–8, prints 'kingdoms' following E. Thompson's edition of *The Works* (1776). The British Library 1681 *Miscellaneous Poems* has 'kingdome'.
5. See Sir W. M. Petty, *The Political Anatomy of Ireland* (1691): 'That Carrickfergus may be always seen from Scotland is well known and but a small boat may row over in 3 or 4 hours is experienced' (p. 110). Irish historians have observed that Great Britain acted positively as 'a barrier between Ireland and the Continent' (e.g. J. C. Beckett, *A Short History of Ireland* (1968) p. 9). Petty saw the English as keeping 'the chain or drawbridge between the two kingdoms on the English side' (*Political Anatomy*, p. 110). An MP in Richard Cromwell's parliament remarked that 'We are one clod of earth. Neptune lashes our shore on every side. We are as in a cockboat. We swim securely while we do not divide', J. T. Rutt (ed.), *The Diary of Thomas Burton M.P.*, 4 vols (1828), Vol. iv, p. 145 (hereafter *Burton's Diary*).
6. G. Burnet, *Memoires of the Dukes of the Hamilton* (1677), *Preface*, Sig. a 2.
7. See W. Haller, *Foxe's Book of Martyrs and the Elect Nation* (London, 1963).
8. A. H. Williamson, *Scottish National Consciousness in the Age of James VI* (Edinburgh, 1979), p. 15.

9. Ibid., p. 145.
10. C. H. Mcllwain (ed.), *Political Works of James I* (Cambridge, Mass., 1918), pp. 271–3.
11. See M. Lee, Jr., *Government by the Pen: Scotland in the Reign of James VI and I* (Urbana, 1980).
12. Polydore Vergil, *Historia Anglia* quoted in R. L. Mackie, *King James IV of Scotland* (Edinburgh, 1958), p. 93.
13. Charles I certainly thought the Covenant anti-monarchical: 'so long as this Covenant is in force . . . I have no more power in Scotland than as a Duke of Venice, which I will rather die than suffer'. Burnet, *Memoires*, pp. 59–61. See also W. Balcanquhal, *A Large Declaration Concerning the Late Tumults in Scotland* (1639). Cf. also Charles's answer to the Nineteen Propositions in 1642.
14. D. Stevenson, *The Scottish Revolution 1637–44* (Newton Abbot, 1973), p. 57. 'Rebel' Agents in London reported sympathy for the Covenant there. The Covenant was not in itself anti-English but opposed rule from England. Charles in fact had kept his English council, apart from a few like Laud, ignorant of his Scottish policies.
15. S. R. Gardiner, *Constitutional Documents of the Puritan Revolution 1625–1660*, 3rd edn (Oxford, 1906), pp. 199–201.
16. Williamson, *Scottish National Consciousness*, pp. 142–6.
17. See also W. Ferguson, *Scotland's Relations with England: A Survey to 1707* (Edinburgh, 1977), p. 127, for the suggestion that there were hopes of a 'reformed international' exciting some interest on the continent. Archibald Johnson of Warington cited in G. Donaldson *Scotland: James V–James VII* (Edinburgh, 1978), p. 332.
18. See e.g. V. Pearl, 'London's Counter-revolution' in G. E. Aylmer (ed.), *The Interregnum* (1972); her 'London Puritans and Scotch Fifth Columnists' in A. J. Hollaender and W. Kellaway, *Studies in London History* (London, 1969); and D. Stevenson, *Revolution and Counter-Revolution in Scotland 1644–1651* (London, 1977), esp. pp. 1–81.
19. Stevenson, *Revolution and Counter-Revolution*, chapters 3 and 4. Charles agreed in the Engagement 'according to the intention of his father' to 'endeavour a complete union of the kingdoms, so as they may be one under his majesty', Gardiner *Constitutional Documents*, p. 351.
20. Stevenson, *Revolution and Counter-Revolution*, p. 129.
21. C. H. Firth (ed.), *The Cromwellian Union* (Edinburgh, 1902), p. 6 n., quoting T. McCrie (ed.), *The Life of Mr Robert Blair* (Woodrow Society, 1848), p. 291.
22. Firth, *Cromwellian Union*, pp. xvii and xxii. See also pp. xviii–xix for references to the need for union as for 'the good of this island' and for 'the good and peace of the people of this island'. C. H Dand, *The Mighty Affair:*

How Scotland lost her Parliament (Edinburgh, 1972), asserts *per contra* that 'all that Cromwell's total union of England and Scotland meant to the English was that the key of her back-door dangled safely from the Protector's belt' (p. 21).

23. Gardiner, *Constitutional Documents*, pp. 414, 418–25. See also I. Roots, 'Cromwell's Ordinances' in Aylmer (ed.), *The Interregnum*, pp. 156–8.

24. Gardiner, *Constitutional Documents*, pp. 447–59; H. Scobell (ed.), *A Collection of Acts and Ordinances* (1658), pp. 389–95.

25. For the Debates see *Burton's Diary*, Vols iii and iv, (reference to a 'treble-cord', Vol. iv, p. 7 and 168, 'provinces' and 'foreigners' Vol. iv, p. 130). E. D. Goldwater, 'The Scottish Franchise: Lobbying during the Cromwellian Protectorate', *Historical Journal*, 21 (1978), pp. 27–42, brings out attitudes to the Scots in 1657.

26. C. H. Firth (ed.), *The Memoirs of Edmund Ludlow*, 2 vols (Oxford, 1894), Vol. i, p. 298.

27. See the reports of Robert Lilburne in C. H. Firth (ed.), *Scotland and the Commonwealth* (Edinburgh, 1895), passim.

28. See F. D. Dow, *Cromwellian Scotland 1651–1660* (Edinburgh, 1979), esp. chapters 5–12, and M. P. Ashley, *General Monck* (London, 1977), esp. chapters 9–15.

29. Firth, *Cromwellian Union*, Appendix of 'Papers relating to the Union Negotiations in 1670', pp. 187–224.

30. J. Swift, 'The Publick Spirit of the Whigs' in H. Davis (ed.), *Political Tracts 1713–1714* (Oxford, 1953), p. 49.

31. See P. H. Scott (ed.), *1707: The Union of Scotland and England* (Edinburgh, 1979), chapters 9 and 10 (pp. 55–67). H. R. Trevor-Roper *Religion, the Reformation and Social Change* (London, 1967), p. 466, sees the 1707 union as 'a revised version of the Cromwellian Union'.

32. See D. B. Quinn, *The Elizabethans and the Irish* (Ithaca, 1966), and N. Canny, *The Elizabethan Conquest of Ireland 1565–1576* (Brighton, 1976), chapter 7.

33. See M. Perceval-Maxwell, *The Scottish Migration to Ulster in the Reign of James I* (Belfast, 1973).

34. See M. Perceval-Maxwell, 'Strafford, the Ulster-Scots and the Covenanters', *Irish Historical Studies*, 18 (1972–3), pp. 524–51; H. F. Kearney, *Strafford in Ireland* (Manchester, 1959).

35. See M. Perceval-Maxwell, 'The Ulster Rebellion of 1641 and the Depositions', *Irish Historical Studies*, 21 (1978), pp. 144–67, esp. 155–65.

36. For reactions in England to the Rebellion see particularly K. S. Bottigheimer, *English Money and Irish Land* (Oxford, 1971), pp. 30–53 and K. J. Lindley, 'The Impact of the 1641 Rebellion upon England and Wales 1641–5', *Irish Historical Studies*, 18 (1972–3), pp. 143–76.

37. See J. Lowe, 'Charles I and the Confederation of Kilkenny 1643–9', *Irish Historical Studies*, 14 (1964), pp. 1–19.
38. See J. L. Malcolm, 'All the King's Men. The Impact of the Crown's Irish Soldiers on the English Civil War', *Irish Historical Studies*, 22 (1979), pp. 239–64. Malcolm cites John, Lord Byron as representative of royalists who felt that since parliament had called the Scots into England there was no reason 'Why the King should make any scruple of calling in the Irish, or the Turks if they would serve him'. See also Lindley, 'Impact', pp. 168–76.
39. The most recent account of the New Model Army is by H. Kishlansky, *The Rise of the New Model Army* (Cambridge, 1979). See also D. Massarella's article *infra*. H. Hazlett has surveyed 'The Financing of the British Armies in Ireland 1644–1649', *Irish Historical Studies*, 1 (1938), pp. 21–41. He notes a 'burst of activity' by parliament in the late 1640s resulting in 'a simplified and more efficient way of bringing in its revenue' without which 'it is doubtful whether even Cromwell's military genius could have forced the decisive action he did in so short a time' (p. 41).
40.   And now the Irish are ashamed
        To see themselves in one year tamed:
        So much one man can do
        That does both act and know . . .
        He to the Commons' feet presents
        A kingdom for his first year's rent
        And what he may, forbears
        His fame, to make it theirs.
        (Donno, *Andrew Marvell*, pp. 56–7)
41. See e.g. Firth, *Ludlow's Memoirs*, passim, and R. G., *A Copy of a Letter from an Officer of the Army in Ireland to his Highness the Lord Protector* (1656; reprint, Exeter, 1974).
42. See T. C. Barnard, *Cromwellian Ireland: English Government and Reform in Ireland 1649–1660* (Oxford, 1975), and 'Planters and Policies in Cromwellian Ireland', *Past and Present*, 61 (1973), pp. 31–69; and Dow, *Cromwellian Scotland*, pp. 161–228.
43. Bottigheimer, *English Money*, p. 3; M. MaCurtain, *Tudor and Stuart Ireland* (Dublin, 1972), pp. 154–160. For details of the Commonwealth Surveys see Y. M. Goblet, *La transformation de la geographie politique de l'Irelande au XVIIe siècle*, 2 vols (Paris, 1930).
44. G. D. Owen (ed.), *H. M. C. Report on the De L'Isle and Dudley MSS.*, Vol. vi (1966), pp. 596–9.
45. *Burton's Diary*, Vols iii and iv, passim.
46. Quoted F. Warner, *The History of the Rebellion and Civil War in Ireland*, (London, 1767), p. 575.
47. Bottigheimer, *English Money*, p. 124.

48. Barnard, *Cromwellian Ireland*, p. 305. See also K. Bottigheimer, 'The Restoration Land Settlement in Ireland', *Irish Historical Studies*, 18 (1972) pp. 1–21.

Postscript

'Union and Disunion' was the outcome of an interest in the peculiar problems of government in early modern multiple or composite kingdoms, notably Hapsburg Spain and Brandenburg Prussia, comparing and contrasting them with the early Stuart inheritance of three kingdoms and a principality. This interest, first developed in lectures given during the 1970s to various historical societies, culminated in the (unpublished) A. H. Dodd Memorial Lecture at the University College of North Wales, Bangor 1977, which urged the profitability of examining what went on between and within the constituents of 'the British Isles' at a time of troubles, a crisis even, for all of them. The article itself, seen as something of a pioneering work,[1] may still have something to say amid the proliferation of books and articles on this period and theme poured out by historians of England, of Scotland, Wales and Ireland, and of combinations of all or some of these, exploring internal developments, relationships with England—the ruler's permanent residence and in other ways, too, a domineering force—and with one another. This last has still not received the attention it deserves. Terms such as 'British History' and 'the New British History' are giving way to 'the British Problem' and to 'the history of the Atlantic Archipelago'.[2] Each demands definition—not easy when coping with an amorphous region without obvious boundaries and put together more by history than geography.

John Morrill, co-founder of a Cambridge Tripos course on 'The British Problem' between two acts of union, one for England and Wales (1534), the other (1707) with Scotland, each achieved by its own peculiar methodology, is editor with his colleague, Brendan Bradshaw, of an enterprising far-ranging collective work, *The British Problem, c. 1534 to 1707* (1996).[3] This is the outcome of an enquiry 'how to conceptualise the relationship' between the kingdoms of England, Scotland, Ireland and Wales, brought to a focus in the dynastic inheritance of Charles I, with all of them interacting in some measure within a periphery from the Channel Islands to the Northern Isles, the whole making up the Atlantic Archipelago. This term, which appears to be a coinage of R. S. Tompson in 1986,[4] has been taken up in response to the expressed susceptibilities of the new Irish historians for whom 'the British Isles' smacks of racial ignorance and colonialism. Sensitive now to this sentiment, I have yet retained for the record the impugned appelation for the reprint of my article of 1981, when it was commonly employed and presumably more acceptable. The 'invincible' hostility to Scotland, expressed, it seems, in my *The Great Rebellion* (1966), was really non-existent,[5] and against any lingering suspicion of chauvinism I declare my increasing admiration for Irish historiography of this period, typified by the innovative collection of articles got together under the editorship of Jane H. Ohlmeyer with the provocative title *Ireland from Independence to Occupation, 1641–1660* (1995), illuminating themes of change and continuity, stressing the distinctiveness of Ireland, not least culturally and economically.[6] The fact remains that there is still no truly satisfactory inclusive yet neutral term to characterise the amorphous area under review. It has to be said that what has given Ireland its part in British history is the determination of so many Irish not to be in any way a part of 'Britain'.

What is certain is that it really will not do to continue the traditional Anglocentricity of so much historical writing on the period. David Cannadine complains that the 'New Oxford History of England', now in process, looks like being no more 'British' than the old series.[7] Ironically, one of the first two volumes to appear, of the New Penguin History of Britain with Cannadine as general editor, covering the seventeenth century, is by Mark Kishlansky, a conspicuous revisionist, who concerns himself with Scotland and Ireland only when they impinge directly on salient English episodes.[8] Wales gets two mentions *en passant*. (For some redress, see Stephen Roberts's chapter *infra*.) The prime cultural achievements of Scotland appear to be the introduction of golf into England by James I and at the end of the century the Bank of Scotland. Surely historians must take account of Irish, Scots and Welsh, not only within the concerns of God's Englishmen, but in their own right, too, and in their relationships with one another. Yet some revisionist history of 'these islands'—a wan alternative to the British Isles—continues to bother with them only because between 1637 and 1641 they stirred up problems which spilled over· to upset a stable England maintaining a practical political consensus. Conrad Russell sees them as a British problem which ensured the dissolution of government (in England) which itself brought on the civil war.[9] Brilliant. Yet not enough, not only for those 'old guard' and 'old hat' historians still not down-and-out, but for the burgeoning cohort of post-revisionists who discern an England before 1640 already moving politically and religiously into polarity. Scotland, and Ireland, particularly, may represent an external contingency disturbing England, but to have an impact the contingent needs something there to implode upon—and there was plenty there in 1640–1. When there was a call to subdue a rebellious 'colony', which both King and parliament were determined to hang on to, raising in a novel form the question of the location of control of armed force, civil war need not have been the outcome, but surely there was bound to be some 'trouble' derived from an existing tension exacerbated. The claim that without the Irish Rebellion 'the normal proesses of compromise and consensus which were at the heart of English politics would have had time to function' seems unduly optimistic. In any case there was more than politics to it. Religion was a divisive force long before, now more than ever.[10]

What the period 1637–42 highlights is the fact that Charles I signally failed as sovereign of a composite kingdom to implement co-ordinated policies across his territories. He was always too ready to think how to divide and rule rather than to weld them into a single entity—a British state identified as such—effectively under control from England. There were certainly drifts towards Anglicanisation—if not colonisation—in Ireland, more under Wentworth than Charles himself could have intended.[11] If later on the Cromwellian conquest under Commonwealth and Protectorate had endured in both Scotland and Ireland such a single unit might have emerged. But the Restoration, while clinching much of the land settlement in Ireland, dispersed more ambitious efforts. While there were discussions later in Charles II's reign about a Scottish union, there was no concerted drive behind them.[12] The internal and external threats to security and order perceived by the regicide republic had not been enough to formulate the identity of 'the united state of Great Britain and Ireland', and when union came with Scotland in 1707, and with Ireland in 1801, its auspices were very different. Scotsmen, Irishmen, Welshmen and Englishmen, to say nothing of Channel Islanders and Shetlanders, have retained their distinctiveness all through, a distinctiveness accommodating diversity within their own nationhoods, Lowlanders and Highlanders in Scotland, for example. In seventeenth-century Ireland there were the native Irish, the Old English, the new English influx, the Ulster Scots. To make a genuinely United Kingdom out of all that lot was unfeasible then, as it has been since. The best any ruler could hope for was something of a firm state within each kingdom. Cromwell may have inadvertently 'cast the kingdom old / Into another mould', but what was poured into it was too volatile to set. A national identity for England was a possibility, actively pursued to the point that it was almost one for the entire area.[13] Anglocentricity has endured unshaken and a 'British' Prime Minister, dead set against devolution for Scotland and Wales, has described the constitution—if there is one—of the United Kingdom as having endured for a thousand years.[14] But we have yet to see a truly British state and until we do there will be no genuinely British history. That lack is, maybe, the British Problem.

Notes

1. For example, by C. Hill, *The English Bible and the Seventeenth-Century Revolution* (Harmondsworth, 1993), p. 34, n. 144.
2. My own 1981 suggestion of 'the general crisis of the British Isles' for the period under review (pp. 20–21 *supra*) has yet to be taken up and no doubt never will be.
3. B. Bradshaw and J. Morrill (eds), *The British Problem, c. 1534–1707: State Formation in the Atlantic Archipelago* (London, 1996). See esp. the Introduction (by Morrill) and J. G. A. Pocock's 'The Atlantic Archipelago and the War of the Three Kingdoms', and D. Hirst's 'The English Republic and the Meaning of Britain'.
4. R. S. Tompson, *The Atlantic Archipelago: A Political History of the British Isles* (Lewiston, 1986). Two other thoughtful general histories of the British Isles are by H. F. Kearney, (Cambridge, 1989) and J. Black, (London, 1966).
5. W. Ferguson, *Scotland's Relations with England* (Edinburgh, 1977), p. 306.
6. J. H. Ohlmeyer (ed.), *Ireland from Independence to Occupation 1641–1660* (Cambridge, 1995). see esp. the 'Introduction: A Failed Revolution?' and the (unduly modesty titled) Select Bibliography.
7. D. Cannadine, 'British History as a New Subject' *Past and Present*, 31 (1992), in A. Grant and K. J. Stringer (eds), *Uniting the Kingdom: The Making of British History*, (London, 1995), ch. 2, pp. 12–28.
8. M. Kishlansky, *A Monarchy Transformed: Britain 1603–1714* (Harmondsworth, 1996).
9. C. Russell, *The Fall of the British Monarchies, 1637–1642* (Oxford, 1991), chapter 10 passim; and *The Causes of the English Civil·War* (Oxford, 1990), esp. chapters 5 and 6.
10. See particularly E. H. Sagan, 'Constructing Discord: Ideology, Propaganda and the English Response to the Irish Rebellion of 1641', *Journal of British Studies*, 36 (1996).

11. N. Canny, 'The Attempted Anglicisation of Ireland in the Seventeenth Century: An example of "British History" ', and J. H. Ohlmeyer, 'Strafford, the Londonderry Business' and the 'New British History' in J. F. Merritt (ed.), *The Political World of Thomas Wentworth, Earl of Strafford 1621– 1641* (Cambridge, 1996).
12. C. S. Terry (ed.), *The Cromwellian Union . . . 1651–1652*, appx. papers relating to Union negotiations in 1670, Scottish Hist. Society (Edinburgh, 1902).
13. D. Hirst, 'The English Republic and the Meaning of Britain', in Bradshaw and Morrill, *The British Problem.*
14. John Major during the 1997 election campaign.

2

Religion, Politics and Welshness, 1649–1660

Stephen Roberts

A recent theme in treatments of the English Revolution of the 1640s and 1650s has been the emphasis on what is sometimes called the 'British dimension'. Professor Ivan Roots in this volume explores the relationship between constituent parts of Britain, and Professor Russell has in two major books constructed a view of the English Civil War as essentially a British war, produced by a crisis of government and a loss of confidence in Charles I by his subjects in the three kingdoms.[1] Wales is conspicuously absent from these discussions. The reason for this is not hard to find: Wales after the 1530s was not a kingdom. In 1603 there had been a union of crowns between Scotland and England, in which Scottish identities were recognised as separate and continuing. Ireland, too, was another kingdom, with the King of England at its head. Under the Instrument of Government of 1653, the paper constitution forming the foundation of the Cromwellian Protectorate, there was a *de facto* union of England with Scotland and Ireland. There was to be one parliament, with Irish and Scottish representation, but separate administrations for the two Celtic countries persisted.[2] The aim of this chapter is to suggest ways in which Wales and the identity of the Welsh were affected by wider developments in the British nations, and by events in England in particular, and to show how the 1650s in this respect, as in so many others, produced new ideas and perceptions. How was 'Welshness' affected by the experience of the Commonwealth and Protectorate?

We have to begin by sketching in some background to Anglo-Welsh relations. The Act of Union of 1536 between England and Wales was of a different order from the seventeenth-century constitutional changes in Scotland and Ireland. As many historians have pointed out, the act might better be described as an Act of Assimilation. The very phrase 'Act of Union' is itself not contemporary; it was coined by the Welsh nationalist scholar Owen M. Edwards in 1901. It implies a surrender of a nation state-hood which did not exist even before 1536. Most scholars now see the act as a codifying and tidying-up exercise. It gave Wales shire government and led to the setting up of the council in the marches of Wales, which, as if to underscore the point that Wales had no existence as a state, extended its jurisdiction into England as far east as Evesham in the county of Worcester.[3]

By the outbreak of the civil war, Wales was in governmental terms simply a region of England. And yet the assimilation was evidently incomplete, and a Welsh identity continued to trouble the tidy-minded. Images of the Welsh in popular literature of the 1640s and 1650s had not moved on from those abounding in Tudor England. The stock caricature of the Welsh drew on their clothes, language, accent, culture and diet for material and ridiculed all of them. The stereotype had been well in place by the time Shakespeare's Fluellin, in *Henry V*, took the stage as a comic but brave and loyal figure. When large numbers of Welsh people joined the King's side during the first civil war, the London presses were able to draw on over a century of imagery with which to pillory the Welsh character. *The Welchmans Life, Death and Periall, The Welchman's Inventory, The Welchman's Declaration, The Welchman's Postures, The Welchmans Complements, The Welchmans Public Recantation, The Welchmans Last Petition* were all titles from 1642–3 ridiculing the royalist Welsh troops in scathing terms. The good humour of Shakespeare's portrayal was absent now that the English were apparently threatened by the Welsh in arms.[4]

The stereotyping of the Welsh continued through the rest of the 1640s and 1650s. In a collection by Alexander Brome of ballads from the years of the 'late troubles', *The Rump, or an Exact Collection of . . . Songs* (1662), the Welsh, garrulous, lousy, poor, cowardly and flatulent, take their place along with other stereotype ballads about the Irish, Scots, Dutch and virtually every other national group. Compared with all of these, of course, the English were bold, resolute and transparently honest. It is possible to attach too much significance to these ephemeral publications. Most were the work of hack journalists who would alter copy to suit whatever circumstances demanded. A book called *The True Copy of a Welch Sermon* appeared in 1643 as a skit on a Welsh parson's comic sermon against Prince Maurice. In 1646 it was reissued, with sections rewritten, as an attack on Princes Rupert and Maurice in the light of the collapse of the royalist cause after Naseby.[5] What had started as an attack on the Welsh had turned into a jeer at the King's defeat. As well as doubts over their integrity, there remains the question of how influential these satires really were. It is difficult to be sure, but a clue may be found in Alexander Brome's preface to *The Rump*. He tells us that many of the songs were written by 'gentlemen', anonymously, when it was not safe to claim authorship. The reference to gentlemen should put us on our guard against too easy an acceptance that this was genuine popular culture.

Of more significance politically was another, more profound dimension of Welshness: the myth of the Welsh as the closest descendants of the ancient British. Based on embroidery by Geoffrey of Monmouth, this was the tale that Brutus and the Trojans had established an empire in these islands which had flourished down to AD 664 and the death of Cadwaladr. The Cymry were the most authentic link with this glorious past. The myth was inseparable from the belief that a chosen son would appear to restore the empire to its former splendour. The literary myth-makers found plenty of material with the accession of Henry Tudor in 1485; he became the 'son of destiny' that the myth demanded. The Welsh link with the Tudors explains, of course, Shakespeare's (and Henry V's) indulgence towards Fluellin. This theory of the descent of the British was generally accepted by scholars and writers, and reached its high water mark under Elizabeth I. It is important to stress that all this was more useful to the English monarchy than to the Welsh people. Around it was created a theory of the descent of the English church to justify the Elizabethan church settlement. From the visit of Joseph of Arimathaea to Britain sprang the Church of England; papal rule was not the real basis of ecclesiastical authority. The most effective literary use of this view of history was by Edmund Spenser. *The Faerie Queene* embodies what some scholars call the 'Galfridian' interpretation (i.e. after Geoffrey of Monmouth) of British history and defends it against the scepticism of Polydore Vergil, the Italian scholar who had become a naturalised Englishman.[6]

The Arthurian legend woven into Geoffrey of Monmouth's history survived the accession of the Stuarts. George Owen Harry produced a genealogy of James I which showed him as a descendant of Owen Tudor through his mother, and thus a Welshman. In fact, James was descended from Henry VII on both his mother's and his father's side, and preferred to derive his Welsh ancestry by emphasising his father's lineage. By the early seventeenth century, however, the problem with the Galfridian/Spenserian myth was that it had become inseparably associated with the monarchy. It had become the stock-in-trade of literary artificers and courtly flatterers, but no longer carried the potency in popular culture which it may have done in Wales during the Middle Ages. The romance of the legend of Brutus was no more generally convincing as a focus for a Welsh identity than the scurrilous caricatures of the London yellow press. The learned antiquarian correspondence of Sir Simonds D'Ewes and the celebrated Welsh antiquary, Dr John Davies of Mallwyd, on the eve of the civil war was in its pious respect for the culture of the Cymry a reminder of this way of seeing Wales, but bore no relation to popular or non-intellectual perceptions of the Welsh.[7]

What is clear from the surviving evidence is that the Welsh were— some would argue still are—a stateless people. 'Wales' may have been abolished as a nation, but the Welsh people were readily identifiable: both by themselves and by observers from outside. From the mid- to late 1640s, as is well-known, parliament turned its attention to the need to establish a preaching ministry in Wales, and authorised a small number of leading Puritan preachers to blaze a trail in Wales ahead of something more permanent. To meet the needs of the 'dark corners of the land', in 1650 the Rump Parliament established the Commission for the Propagation of the Gospel in Wales, which became not only the powerhouse for an evangelical itinerant Puritan ministry, but, it has been argued, the real government of Wales.[8]

The Commission for the Propagation of the Gospel was the most distinctive innovation by the state in Welsh ecclesiastical and secular government in the 1650s. Before we consider its impact on perceptions of Welshness, we need to remind ourselves what the commission actually did. It was organised into two sides, lay and clerical, and had separate sub-committees for North and South Wales, themselves divided into county groups. It employed a group of paid officials—twenty in Glamorgan alone worked for the commission between 1650 and 1653— who had previously been sequestrators of royalists' estates or minor functionaries elsewhere in the service of the local state. Treasurers for different regions of the counties collected money from tithe farmers. The latter were laymen who paid the commissioners an annual predetermined rent, and then themselves collected tithes, either in kind or in money payments, from tithepayers in the parishes. The tithes that were targeted had belonged to royalist lay impropriators, deans and chapters of cathedrals, livings once held by the crown and by clergymen ejected from their parishes for supporting the King or for what was called 'insufficiency' or 'scandalous living'. Most of the tithes paid in any Welsh county thus passed to the commissioners, who then funded a team of itinerant preachers. It is important to remember that the itinerants were not the only ministers in Wales during the years that the propagation commission was in force. In South Wales 196 ministers were ejected from their livings by the commissioners, but 127 were pronounced to be satisfactory. Some eighty-two were ejected in the north, and fewer survived the scrutiny of the commissioners than in the south. Dr A. M. Johnson has calculated that there were around ninety itinerants in Wales from 1650 to 1653, replacing those ejected.[9]

The reputation of the commission as providing the dynamic of government in Wales rests on several features of its work. First, the centrality of tithepaying in seventeenth-century life, and especially the vested interest of the gentry as the beneficiaries of tithes, ensured that any attempt to alter the basis of this aspect of the tax system was bound to be seen as a radical change. Reformers in successive parliaments debated tithes repeatedly, and the subject was a major theme in controversies about the future direction of the Commonwealth. Oliver Cromwell was all for tithe reform in 1650, but by 1654 had become convinced that no state church could be sustained without maintaining the tithe system. In a recent discussion of whether radical solutions to the political and religious problems of England and Wales could have been implemented in the 1650s, G. E. Aylmer suggests that a compromise might have been found between outright abolition of tithes and the maintenance of the status quo. There was nothing inevitable about the failure of radical reform in the 1650s, he says; 'might not some compromise not have been possible for the commutation or amortisation of tithes?'[10] It not only was a possibility: it was what was actually happening in Wales between 1650 and 1653, because the propagators and their officials put a fixed annual value on tithes in parishes. This tended to speed up the transition from payments in kind to money payments, and in some places regularised what was a notoriously

34

localised and customary system. The radical dimension in the work of the propagation commission will be discussed further below.

Another feature of the commissioners' work which has been commented on by many historians is their work in the field of education. Thomas Richards, writing in 1920, fully unveiled the extent to which schools were set up in Wales under this scheme: thirty-seven were organised in the south and twenty-six in the north.[11] More remains to be said about these schools; the evidence largely turns on details we have of appointments of schoolmasters. A schoolmaster appointed does not necessarily mean a school set up, and we know virtually nothing about the schools themselves. On the other hand, we now know that Thomas Richards underestimated somewhat the number of schoolmasters appointed; more names have come to light since he wrote over seventy years ago. The motive for setting up these schools was religious, of course: pupils who could read, could read the Scriptures. There are hints that these schools were open to all: Roger Seys was approved as schoolmaster at St Fagans and was to teach 'all such children' as came to the school. Other schools were described as 'free'. The curriculum gives no comfort to those looking for support for the Welsh language; in Lampeter a school was set up in 1652 'for the educacon of youthes in English and Latine tongue'; in 1651 Ambrose Lewis was recommended as a master at Wrexham to teach scholars 'in Latin and Greek tongue'.[12]

A third theme in the case for viewing the commission as central as an agency of government is its involvement in purely secular matters. Dr Johnson has discovered that the commissioners acted as an indemnity committee for Wales, discussing cases of soldiers seeking indemnity for their actions during the civil war.[13] It is this secular work of the commissioners, significant though it was, which is easily inflated at the expense of a proper regard for the other, continuing agencies of government in Wales. The courts of great sessions, county courts of quarter sessions, the customs and excise establishments (new since 1643), all continued in Wales to provide the backbone of secular government. It is true that it is very difficult to distinguish the county committees from the county sub-committees of the propagation commission, but in the 1650s committee rule—over the estates of royalist delinquents, for example—was in long-term decline, despite the reopening of cases under the major-generals, in 1655.

After the failure of the Rump Parliament to renew the propagation commission in 1653, Cromwell invited the commissioners to carry on under his authority until some other system was established, and from 1654 a new body, the Commission for the Approbation of Public Preachers, was set up in London to vet new appointments to the church. They were known as the 'triers', and they were assisted by local committees who continued the work of ejecting unsatisfactory ministers. These 'ejectors' were organised in England on a county by county basis, but in Wales were grouped into a committee for the north and one for the south, thus maintaining some of the structure of the propagation commission. In fact down to 1660 there was a great deal of continuity of personnel between the system pre- and post-1654, and after 1660 laymen continued to speak of the Commission for the Propagation of the Gospel as behind events taking place in 1657 or 1658, even though the commission was formally wound up in 1653.[14]

What, then, were the implications of the propagation experiment for the elusive subject of Welsh identity? Thomas Richards, writing as a Welsh-speaking Welsh Baptist, described the scheme as 'thoroughly English' in essence, since it originated in the London parliament and empowered commissioners led by the English radical, Colonel Thomas Harrison. Yet the subject is more complex than this. Certainly the background was one in which contemporaries on either side of Offa's Dyke saw the Welsh as poor and benighted: poor economically, poor spiritually, poor morally and poor, exciting pity. Cromwell spoke of the 'poor people of God' in Wales; to Major-General Berry, set over the Welsh in 1655, they were 'a poor people, who have suffered much'. In sermons before parliament from 1646 onwards, preachers like Walter Cradock, a leading Independent minister, pleaded lest 'poor Wales continue sighing, famishing, mourning and bleeding'. When John Byrd, the customs collector of South Wales, sent his brother-in-law in England two cheeses and a dolphin boxed up as a gift, he described it in his covering note as a 'poor token from Wales'.[15] It was perhaps this vision of Wales which commanded more general consent than either what had become the irrelevancies of Arthurian mythology or the absurdities of the gutter press, though views on the poverty of the Welsh could easily shade into derision. Major-General Berry, basically sympathetic, writing to John Thurloe in 1656, said that the Welsh were 'an affectionate tender-spirited people that want judgment: they live farre of, and want information'. William Richards, in a 1682 book called *Wallography, or the Britton Describ'd*, asserted that the Welsh were 'a rude people and want much instruction'. Richards was like the twentieth-century novelist

Caradoc Evans, who also pilloried the Welsh character, writing as an outsider in his own society, but he was a perpetuator of a tradition of ridicule that went back 150 years and more.[16]

So did the propagators themselves, who were mostly Welsh, despite the presence among them of Englishmen, see themselves as bringing the benefits of English power to Wales as they built up their preaching ministry? In my view, the commissioners, with one notable exception, did see themselves as agents of a victorious English parliament, which had received a special dispensation from God to inaugurate God's kingdom on earth. In the actions and correspondence of men like Colonel John Jones, a lay commissioner who was one of the leading figures in Ireland during the Commonwealth, or Colonel Philip Jones, a busy committeeman often credited with being 'virtually ruler of South Wales',[17] or even Vavasor Powell, the leading figure in the implementation of the evangelising side of the propagators' work, there is little to suggest a developing or developed sense of Welshness. Powell spent much time in London, among London congregations, and preached sermons to the fathers of the City of London on the way forward for the godly. Philip Jones became the major-domo of Cromwell's household in London. There was a strong element of London Welshness among these men, and much of their public behaviour was conditioned by what went on in the churches, councils and parliaments of the capital.

The exceptional figure among the commissioners, mentioned earlier, was Morgan Llwyd, 'Morgan Llwyd o Wynedd' to Welsh *litterateurs*. Llwyd was a minister, so far as we know never ordained in Anglican holy orders, who had been influenced by other leaders of the Welsh separatist Puritan movement, and had moved around England during the 1640s, probably with the parliamentary armies, before ending up at Wrexham as a minister to a gathered church there. He died in 1659 at the age of forty. He was exceptional for a number of reasons. For one thing he wrote a significant number of works in the Welsh language during the 1650s, while most of his contemporaries wrote in English. Of Llwyd's published works, eight are in Welsh, three in English. Of these, some were published in London, and some in Dublin, itself a comment on the absence of a significant publishing trade in Wales before 1660. His choice of language was certainly not determined by a greater facility in one than the other. When most of the self-styled Saints in Wales used English as their natural medium for the printed word, even when their preaching was in Welsh, Llwyd's mission was to reach the

Welsh people with books in the language they themselves used in everyday speech. He was trying to speak directly to the Welsh people and to engage in dialogue with their culture, the culture of the *gwerin*, the folk or ordinary people.[18]

Like others among the propagators, Llwyd saw himself as living in the last days. The execution of Charles I was the crucial event which was ushering in the golden age. Llwyd wrote much prophetic verse, mostly in English interestingly, that linked biblical prophecy, in Daniel and Revelation and elsewhere in the Bible, to events in his own time. This public verse, verse concerned with events in the public sphere, Llwyd found easiest to write in English. These poems about public events were never published in his own time, nor is there any evidence that they were intended for publication.[19] It is when he wants to address or help the spiritual condition of the Welsh, as when casting the psalms into metrical verse, or counselling people to turn from wickedness, that Llwyd turns to the Welsh language. Llwyd is passionately devoted to the plight of the Welsh people. He sees them, as did the other propagators, as needing instruction. He declared himself 'ashamed to discover the nakedness of Wales' and thought that 'the land of our nativitie is asleep'. Wales as a sleeper, or as a potentially fertile but for the moment childless woman, are two of the images Llwyd uses in his writings addressed to the Welsh. The Bible is the one vital source that he returns to time and again for his imagery; his notebook jottings reveal the complexity of his mind, influenced as it was by the German mystic writer, Jacob Boehme.[20] A lesser but significant source of his imagery is Geoffrey of Monmouth's interpretation of British history, stripped now by Llwyd of its monarchical overtones. Llwyd disregards the association between the Tudors, the Stuarts and the British. He overlooks, too, the work of the Spenserians who had derived the authority of the Elizabethan Church of England from the same roots. Llwyd retains the idea of the Welsh as having had a distinguished and special past: 'This was the island that accepted the gospel first in the time of Lles, son of Coel. Here, some say, Helen was born and her son Constantine. Welshmen, say others, discovered America first. Britons have stood until death for the true faith.'[21]

While accepting and promoting this aspect of the Welsh identity and cultural inheritance, Llwyd repudiates the Welsh preoccupation with genealogy. 'Pedigrees of families are but a web woven by nature in which the spider of pride is lurking', he wrote in Welsh. 'You are nothing, even if you come from the princes of Wales, unless you are of the seed of the prince of the kings of the earth, born, not of the will of man but of the incorruptible seed.' In verse he sang: 'It is easy to break the bow of our fathers/it has long since dried out/some [bows] were flexible in their day /everything dries out with use'.[22]

By the 'bow of our fathers' Llwyd has in mind atavistic, backward-looking values. The faith he promotes he sees as modern, and it is of course the faith of the commissioners for the propagation of the gospel. Here is therefore an apparent paradox: he is urging on to the Welsh the Cambro-British mythology promoted by the Tudors, but declares war on certain values thought to be fundamental to the Welsh identity. Genealogy had been an important measure of gentility in an era when Welsh gentry were poorer than their English counterparts, but with the advent of English law in Wales, genealogical studies became of less practical importance in matters of inheritance. Genealogy could remain a significant aspect of cultural status in Wales, but by the mid-seventeenth century many commentators would remain unimpressed by a long and complex family tree. Morgan Llwyd seems here to be swimming with the tide of modernity.[23]

This is as far as Llwyd's concept of Welshness goes, as profound a writer as he is. His deep sympathy with the Welsh people informed his vocation as a writer. His colleague, with whom he was to have an uneasy relationship in his last years, Vavasor Powell, declared he would rather have preached one sermon than have printed a thousand books. His works are really sermons in print; Llwyd's are examples of the writer's rather than the preacher's craft. Addressing as he does the Welsh people, one might have expected Llwyd to have gone deeper into the subject of Welshness. Another preacher and writer of the time, William Erbery, does so. Llwyd was a North Walian, Erbery a South Walian; Llwyd was fluent in both English and Welsh, Erbery only in English (though he did understand Welsh). The two men knew each other and were friends; Llwyd was a generation younger than Erbery and had been his pupil. Both had antinomian tendencies, being against formalism in religion, and both were sympathetic to the kinds of ideas held by the Quakers from the early 1650s. But one major difference between them was in their attitude to the propagation. Llwyd was involved with the Commission for the Propagation of the Gospel as an approver of itinerant ministers and of schoolmasters. Erbery was a paid itinerant preacher in South Wales during 1650 and 1651 but then broke with his employers on grounds of conscience. He rejected tithes completely, on the grounds that they were wrung from the poor:

> Oh how Paul's care for the churches doth tear the pastors and teachers in pieces, who run from parish to parish, from place to place, from lectures and livings, not considering how their maintenance comes in through the bowels of the poor, from the empty bellies and sweat of hard-labouring men.

From 1652 until his death in 1654 Erbery moved in an increasingly radical direction, finally rejecting the idea of the gathered church, that is, the idea of formal church membership, altogether. He rejected the ministry of the propagators as formalistic, based on a literal and mechanical reliance on Scripture; the true gospel for Erbery was more figurative, more allusive, more mystical. By 1653 Erbery was preaching the holiness of those he called 'scattered Saints', individual Christians responding to God's call within them. This was virtually the same doctrine or anti-doctrine held by the Quakers. Within this theological freedom, Erbery develops an eschatology based on the destiny of Wales. He assumes much of the Galfridian myth: 'Lucius the first Christian king was a Britain; and Contanstine [sic] the great, the first Christian emperour in the world, was a britain or Welshman'.[24] Erbery repeats the view of some (implying slight scepticism, perhaps) that 'Britaines' were 'of the Jews' and says that the English, Dutch and Germans are of the gentiles. Their 'love to the earth' or materialism was 'pure gentilism', says Erbery, alluding to the Sermon on the Mount. He grafts his own appreciation of the Last Days on to this historical mythology to arrive at the idea that the glory of God will first be manifest in the British Isles because they were the first to acknowledge Christ, and allots to each constituent part of the British Isles their historic role. 'I say prelacy fell first by the Scots, Presbytery by the English, Independents and Anabaptists will by the Wesh at last.' Both Christ and antichrist will appear with synods and councils in Wales. All church types will soon fall 'and first in Wales'. Erbery in the dogdays of the propagation experiment saw the failure of the gathered churches in Wales to prosper, and prophesied not decline and recriminations among the godly, but greater glory to come from Wales, 'a wing of great Britain, the greatest isle of the world, where will be the city of the great king'. Erbery looked for great things from the oppressed; Scotland was another specially favoured land, and in a lively appreciation of the social discrimination that prevailed in his society, he gloried in preaching and prophesying by women and by private soldiers.[25]

Erbery was of course on the radical fringe, and was not alone in fusing the mythology of the British with contemporary events; Arise Evans, a London Welshman, did the same and came to a virtually opposite conclusion: that the Stuarts retained the chosen status previously accorded to them by literary-minded courtiers.[26] In Erbery's reading, Galfridian history would be worked out in the Welsh people themselves, an oppressed people not in a formal state. It may seem strange that Erbery was alone in pursuing this theme. What was it that prevented Morgan Llwyd, Vavasor Powell and others from following this path of interpretation? We certainly have to recognise the essentially English derivation of the power that the propagation commissioners and their associates enjoyed, and their acceptance of tithes, albeit in the radically modified form of tithe administration promoted between 1650 and 1653. Erbery's rejection of tithes and of the state's mechanism for ensuring that the gospel was preached in Wales seems to have liberated him at the same time from any sense of allegiance to England.

Even more important than this, however, is the concept of godliness being developed in England during the 1650s, which had profound implications for all in the mainstream of public discourse. In the half century before 1650 there developed in expositions of public morality a distinction between the realm of the public and that of the private. Professor Joel Hurstfield considered that the two were concepts not easily separated in the Elizabethan period, but although in empirical cases it may have been hard to draw hard and fast distinctions it is clear that contemporaries knew or thought they knew the difference.[27] In public life those who put the interest of the public first were to be applauded, those who were out for private ends to be condemned. In public sermons on state occasions, such as assizes, quarter sessions and City of London feasts, preachers dwelt on this basic split between the realm of the public and that of the private, but from the late 1640s, and especially in the 1650s, some preachers, those of the separatist tendency, were redefining this orthodox distinction.[28] The relationship that preoccupied many commentators was the tripartite one between the public, the private and the people of God. The preacher Thomas Horton equated 'the publique' with the people of God but implied he did not mean by that everyone in the nation. Henry Symons exhorted magistrates to protect 'the people of God': 'you should dance God's darlings in your arms and dandle them on your knees'. In sermons preached to parliament in the 1650s, John Owen described God's people as 'the poor preserved remnant', 'a separated people'. It was the duty of the remnant to establish Zion for the benefit of God's people as a whole. Owen warns against those who separate themselves 'from the public interest of the people of God'. Everyone should be able to give an account of their work in founding Zion, and should not become private self-seekers. In another sermon Owen, Oliver Cromwell's chaplain, spoke of God's remnant as 'the seed of Jacob . . . the hidden people'.[29]

Ways of reconciling the old public/private distinction with the concept of the separatist church was one which bedevilled public discourse through the 1650s, and contributed significantly to bitter recriminations during 1655–7 over the legitimacy of the Cromwellian Protectorate. A book by William Sedgwick called *Animadversions upon a letter and paper first sent to His Highness by certain gentlemen out of Wales* appeared in 1656 in response to an attack by Vavasor Powell and other ex-propagators on Oliver Cromwell. Sedgwick's book has recently been characterised by John Morrill as an 'even-handed review of the Protector and his government' but it was much more urgent than that.[30] I hope to show in greater detail elsewhere that Sedgwick was attempting a reconciliation of the tensions between the godly remnant and the ungodly nation, between the view of Cromwell on the one hand as the public soldier and on the other as the private citizen choosing public civil office. Sedgwick's conclusion is Machiavellian; people should accept the status quo because a mix of godly and ungodly is better than rule by intolerant Saints who would be unacceptable to the country as a whole. Political stability has to be considered a priority, even though the country in general, Wales and England, continues to be unregenerate or ungodly.

For those who were most prominent in public affairs in Wales during the 1650s, debates over the definition of the godly and their relationship with the nations of Britain, or the state as a whole, retarded any further development of a Welsh identity. For separatists the problem was one of church membership and was necessarily a problem of defining an exclusive group of individuals, not a national one. Who was to be admitted to the Eucharist or the Lord's Supper as they called it? It was those who had separated from the world who were to be admitted to the Lord's Supper, those who had satisfied the elders of their church of their sanctity. The gulf in the minds of the propagators between sainthood and the 'poor' Welsh people as a whole was unbridgeable. The propagators also had to fight a continuous war of attrition with local critics who accused them of every sort of political corruption. Both the English context of public discourse about the godly and the state, and the local Welsh context of defensive self-justification, prevented any identification between the godly and the Welsh people. Those outside the state system were untrammelled; William Erbery could, in the context of the primacy of the individual scattered believer, make what claims he liked about the Welsh and their potential godliness. In similar vein, when the first Quaker emissaries visited Wales they were strikingly successful in their impact, being received with courtesy and interest by the kind of magistrates who were active persecutors in England. William Erbery and his Quaker successors waged no war on the culture of the people; their theology allowed for acceptance of people as they were. What is interesting about the Quakers in the context of the identity of the Welsh is how they uncompromisingly rejected the reality of differences between languages. 'All languages are to be no more than dust', George Fox wrote as a spokesman for God; languages are 'no more than men learn to dress a horse or women to sweep a house as to divine things'.[31] Here the Quakers had much in common with Morgan Llwyd, who thought that different languages emerged as a consequence of pride and self having shattered the first single common human tongue; there is no shred of cultural nationalism to be found in Llwyd's outlook.

For antinomians, those who rejected formalism of any kind in religion, in England and Wales all paths led to Quakerism. For those like Vavasor Powell, who believed in the idea of using tithes to promote a state safety-net church, to catch those souls who were not yet 'visible saints', the period from 1654 seemed increasingly bleak and threatening, and 1660 was a disaster which overwhelmed them. Between 1660 and his death in 1670, Vavasor Powell spent much of his time in prison; he looked out one day from his cell in Welshpool and saw Richard Davies, an up-and-coming Quaker leader, walking by. 'Behold Zacharias and Elizabeth!' he said to his fellow-prisoner.[32] They in Luke's gospel had walked 'in all the commandments and ordinances of the Lord blameless'; who knows now with what sarcasm or genuine admiration Powell invested those words, but they seem to admit that a future if not *the* future lay with the Friends. The fate of the Welsh propagators was wholly yoked to that of the English republican regimes; for that reason the history of religion, politics and Welshness in 1649–60 cannot be understood in isolation from events in London.

And yet this should not be the last word. Events in Wales, in their turn, had a significant effect on English polity. Cromwell's hopes and disappointments rose and fell with the fate of the propagation experiment, in which he invested much personal emotional capital. The perspectives of the ex-propagators fed into and helped shape the changing language of public discourse about the state after 1655. I have had space only to hint at it here, but the relationship between Wales and England was itself being contested through the 1650s, in long-running allegations of corruption among prominent figures in Welsh public life and in the counter attempts by Morgan Llwyd to recover something of a separate Welsh identity, however limited, in his writings. For the modern historian, Gwyn A. Williams, pursuing a Gramscian line of interpretation, Tudor humanists like Dr John Dee deserve to be called 'organic intellectuals' of the gentry class because they 'were the first Welsh intellectuals fully to enter an English language cultural universe through a British identity'.[33] Seventy years after Dee wrote his *Famous and Rich Discoveries*, we find another attempt to reappraise Welshness. Even though language itself was often seen by them as no more than an obstacle, the attempts of Morgan Llwyd and William Erbery to confront the situation of the Welsh people qualify them—if only them—for consideration as organic intellectuals of the *gwerin*.

Notes

1. C. Russell, *The Causes of the English Civil War* (Oxford, 1990); idem, *The Fall of the British Monarchies 1637–42* (Oxford, 1991). For a useful commentary on Russell's views, in the context specifically of the causes of the civil wars, see Ann Hughes, *The Causes of the English Civil War* (London, 1991), especially pp. 36–61.
2. For an imaginative treatment of the whole subject of relationships between the British nations in the early modern period, see H. Kearney, *The British Isles* (Cambridge, 1989), chapter 7.
3. For an up-to-date survey of recent writing on Anglo-Welsh relations in the sixteenth century, see J. G. Jones, *Early Modern Wales, c. 1625–1640* (Cardiff, 1994), esp. chapters 2 and 3.
4. These are titles of satirical prints noted in F. G. Stephens and M. D. George, *Catalogue of Political and Personal Satires preserved in the Department of Prints and Drawings in the British Museum*, 11 vols (London, 1870–1954).

5. *The True Copy of a Welch Sermon Preached before Prince Maurice in Wales
   . . . by Sion ap Owen, Priest* (1643); *A True Copy of the Welch Sermon
   Preached before the Two Princes* (1646).
6. G. Williams, *Recovery, Reorientation and Reformation. Wales c. 1415–1642*
   (Oxford, 1987), pp. 439–40, 451–61; Jones, *Early Modern Wales*, pp.
   153–4.
7. E. Owen and G. H. Jones (eds), 'Correspondence between Dr. John Davies
   of Mallwyd and Sir Simonds D'Ewes', *Y Cymmrodor*, 17 (1904).
8. G. H. Jenkins, *The Foundations of Modern Wales 1642–1780* (Oxford,
   1987), chapter 2 passim is a first rate summary of writing on this topic.
9. A. M. Johnson, 'Wales During the Commonwealth and Protectorate' in D.
   H. Pennington and K. V. Thomas (eds), *Puritans and Revolutionaries*
   (Oxford, 1978), p. 238.
10. G. E. Aylmer, 'Collective Mentalities in Mid Seventeenth-Century England:
    III. Varieties of Radicalism', *Transactions of the Royal Historical Society*,
    5th series, 38 (1988), p. 22.
11. T. Richards, *A History of the Puritan Movement in Wales* (London, 1920),
    pp. 222–34.
12. Examples from Lambeth Palace Library, Comm. VIII/1, copy order books
    of the Commissioners for Propagation of the Gospel.
13. Johnson, 'Wales During the Commonwealth', pp. 239–40.
14. For a survey of continuity and change in one county, S. K. Roberts,
    'Godliness and Government in Glamorgan, 1647–1660' in C. Jones, M.
    Newitt, S. Roberts (eds), *Politics and People in Revolutionary England*
    (Oxford, 1986), pp. 225–52.
15. I. Roots (ed.), *Speeches of Oliver Cromwell* (London, 1989) p. 15; T. Birch
    (ed.), *State Papers of John Thurloe*, 7 vols (1742), Vol. iv, p. 582; Walter
    Cradock, quoted in T. Rees, *History of Protestant Nonconformity in Wales*,
    2nd edn (1883), p. 68; Glamorgan Record Office, CL/MS 4.266, Letter Book
    of John Byrd, p. 43. I am preparing for publication an edition of Byrd's
    letter book.
16. *Thurloe State Papers*, Vol. iv, p. 394; W[illiam] R[ichards], *Wallography,
    or the Britton Describ'd* (1682), p. 80.
17. Jenkins, *Foundations of Modern Wales*, p. 39; A. H. Dodd, *Studies in Stuart
    Wales*, 2nd edn (Cardiff, 1971), chapter 4.
18. Llwyd's English and Welsh works and correspondence, now happily all
    published, may be found in *Gweithiau Morgan Llwyd*, Vol. i (ed. T. E. Ellis,
    Bangor and London, 1899); Vol. ii (ed. J. H. Davies, Bangor and London,
    1908), Vol. iii (ed J. G. Jones and G. W. Owen, Cardiff, 1994). For an
    introduction to his work, M. W. Thomas, *Morgan Llwyd* (Cardiff, 1984).
19. Most of these verses on public events may be found in *Gweithiau*, Vol. i.
20. The notebook writings are in *Gweithiau*, Vol. iii, pp. 204–10.

21. *Gweithiau*, Vol. i, p. 185; all translations from the Welsh are my own.
22. *Gweithiau*, Vol. i, p. 214; p. 40.
23. Jones, *Early Modern Wales*, pp. 12–14; idem, *Concepts of Order and Gentility in Wales, 1540–1640* (Llandysul, 1992), pp. 25–7, 59–65, 248–56.
24. W. Erbery, *The Welsh Curate: Or, Paul's Care of All the Churches* (1652), p. 12; idem, *Apocrypha. The Second Epistle of Paul to the Church of Laodicea* (1652), p. 6. For a recent biography of Erbery, B. Ll. James, 'The Evolution of a Radical: The Life and Career of William Erbery (1604–54)', *Journal of Welsh Ecclesiastical History*, 3 (1986), pp. 31–48.
25. William Erbery, *Apocrypha*, pp. 2, 7, 11; idem, *A Flash of Lightning From the East* (1653), preface, sig. O, O2.
26. C. Hill, 'Arise Evans: Welshman in London' in *Change and Continuity in 17th Century England* (London, 1974), pp. 48–77.
27. J. Hurstfield, 'Political Corruption in Early Modern England', *History*, 52 (1967), pp. 16–34.
28. I have in preparation a fuller study of Anglo-Welsh relations which draws on sermons in which the 'public/private' relationship is discussed.
29. T. Horton, *The Safety of Jerusalem Exprest* (1657), p. 7; H. Symons, *A Beautifull Swan with Two Black Feet. Or Magistrates, Deity attended with Mortality and Misery* (1658), p. 22 (I owe this reference to Dr Newton Key); J. Owen, 'God's Work in Founding Zion', in *The Works of John Owen*, ed W. H. Goold, 16 vols (1850–3), Vol. viii, pp. 406–8; 1God's Presence with a People the Spring of their Prosperity', in *Works*, Vol. viii, p. 451.
30. J. S. Morrill, 'Cromwell and his Contemporaries' in Morrill (ed.), *Oliver Cromwell and the English Revolution* (London, 1990), pp. 269–70.
31. G. Fox, J. Stubs, B. Furly, *A Battle-Door For Teachers and Professors to Learn Singular and Plural* (1660), sig. A2; Llwyd, *Gweithiau*, Vol. ii, p. 93. For a subtle treatment of the relations between Llwyd and the Quakers, G. F. Nuttall, *The Welsh Saints 1640–1660* (Cardiff, 1957), chapter iv. Fox's journeys in Wales may be followed in J. L. Nickalls, *Journal of George Fox* (London, 1952).
32. R. Davies, *An Account of the Convincement, Exercises, Services and Travels of . . . Richard Davies* (Philadelphia, 1752), p. 70.
33. G. A. Williams, *The Welsh in their History* (Cardiff, 1982), pp. 25–9.

3

Local Government Reform in England and Wales during the Interregnum

Stephen Roberts

Civil War historians and the government of localities

The history of local government in mid-seventeenth century England and Wales has been something of a sacrifice to historiographical conflict. It is a problem which has attracted interest only since the turn of the century and its slender bibliography has endowed it with little resistance to grander themes. Macaulay was interested in local matters only as a backcloth to an epic and even S. R. Gardiner, penetrating as all his judgements were, offered no interpretation of local institutional change. J. R. Tanner, it is true, considered the justice of the peace but only as a monument to Tudor 'constructive genius', as a symptom of a 'centralised administration'. Early socialist historians took up the theme of the centralised state as a check on the local landed gentry, whose innate acquisitiveness would naturally break forth at any opportunity. E. M. Leonard described the endeavours of Laud and Strafford in the field of poor relief as 'remarkable for more continuous effort to enforce socialistic measures than has been made by the central government of any other great European country'.[1] The 'Puritan Revolution', by contrast, was a victory for bourgeois self-interest. Suspicion of local oligarchies, one presumes, would not have been shared by the great nineteenth-century Liberals, for whom 'local self-government' was a watchword elevated to a political philosophy. Macaulay, after all, had reluctantly condemned the Protectorate as a despotism 'moderated only by the wisdom, the sobriety and the magnanimity of the despot'.[2] There might be differences over whether local self-government was or was not beneficial, but socialists and Whigs could broadly agree that local government was under the control of the centralised state until the civil war, when collapse was succeeded by relaxed central supervision.

More recently, those who have studied local administration directly have endorsed the findings of Sidney and Beatrice Webb, who emphasised the tightened grip of JPs on county institutions. This interpretation, with its respectable if short-lived pedigree, was accommodated by later views. Trevor-Roper's 'revolt of the provinces' against a centralising Renaissance monarchy accords well with a view of 1660 as making no significant difference to the relationship between 'the state' and 'society'. Central government control was over and had been ended probably in 1641. However stimulating Trevor-Roper's work, it needed to be substantiated by more local research and it was Alan Everitt who took up the theme of 'centralisation', reversed it and introduced the concept of an England before the civil war as a federation of 'county communities', provoked into war by the ineptitude and successive encroachments of Charles I and his ministers. For Everitt the Commonwealth and Protectorate were simply part of 'a series of centralising governments', in David Underdown's words.[3] Underdown himself has seen in the Protectorate not fully-blown centralisation, but forces tending to accommodation with the localities, to 'settlement' and to centralisation, each striving for mastery in the country, and each personified in the character and aims of Oliver Cromwell himself.

These debates over the significance of the civil war in the localities have, on the whole, eschewed the study of local institutions. The intrusive county committees are the exception but their significance has been over-stated; they were reformed in the early 1650s and the remaining militia and assessments committees were hardly more powerful than the early Stuart subsidy and lieutenancy commissions. No one could deny that county committees injected a measure of central direction into local affairs; more than that, they were in some places the only institution, once war had broken out, between the localities and anarchy. The concept of the 'county community' as the expression of gentry power has been fought both for and against but these battles have naturally been focused on the 1640s. We await Dr Morrill's sequel to *The Revolt of the Provinces: Conservatives and Radicals in the English Civil War 1630–1650* but his researches into the history of Cheshire during the

Interregnum suggest that he considers the extension of initiatives at parish level to be one important feature of the reconstruction. The Interregnum has been treated most directly by David Underdown, whose *Pride's Purge* and essay on 'Settlement in the Counties' have surveyed the Commonwealth and Protectorate broadly but with great insight. The emphasis has, however, been more on personnel than on structure, more on participation than on performance.

'Centralisation' has been the key in debates on changes in local government. Everitt and Underdown would agree that 'revolutionary governments are usually centralising governments' and would differ only on the extent of the process. But it is not simply a question of how far 'centralisation' *qua* 'alienation-of-the-gentry' was allowed to proceed. Here are some random examples of how inadequate the concept of the centralising state could be. In Glamorgan, the county committee, originally the agent of Whitehall, became impenetrable to outside authority and became a bulwark of localism. The excise regulations of the Rump developed formal administrative procedures but involved devolution to local officeholders on a scale significant enough to allow Sir Roger Twysden of Kent to make payment arrangements with the excise office largely on his own terms. Major-Generals James Berry and Robert Lilburne found that excisemen were deviant localists and implored Secretary Thurloe to 'be careful in disposing powers and places to put them into good hands or you undo us'. Finally, in Cheshire we find the 'godly', including ministers intruded by central committee, establishing parish vestries to increase local administrative initiatives on, for example, alehouse reform. We might do well to heed the apposite (but not succinct) words of a specialist on modern bureaucracies:

> A realistic analysis of centralisation must include a study of the allocation of decisions in the organisation and the methods of influence that are employed by the higher levels to affect the decisions at the lower levels.[4]

The 'methods of influence' used by central governments in the 1650s are still unstudied. Professor Roots's comment in 1972 that work on how ordinances were implemented 'has hardly been attempted' remains true today.[5]

Contemporaries would not have understood the term 'centralisation' in our sense. This is not to imply that the concept is necessarily invalid, of course: Oliver Cromwell would have puzzled to learn that he led a 'bourgeois revolution' but modern historians have found that idea useful in revaluing the 'Great Rebellion'. But what does have considerable import is the apparent lack of a mid-seventeenth-century notion of 'local government'. Most historians have assumed a dichotomy in government between central and local matters, and the commission of the peace is generally used as a frontier of local government *vis-à-vis* the centre. There might, however, be reason to doubt these assumptions.

The fact that the *Oxford English Dictionary* finds no usage of 'local' as meaning 'pertaining to a particular locality', as against 'central', before 1688—and that a New England usage—is not necessarily a difficulty. What is more striking is the consensus among political theorists about the shared responsibilities of government and governed which attached no significance to local rights or independence. Men spoke figuratively of 'commonwealths' at the most intimately local levels. Sir Thomas Smith described parish government as for 'men which doe not rule', and John Norden wrote that a manor was a 'little commonwealth whereof the tenants . . . are the members, the land the body and the lord the head'.[6] They spoke with some justification since customary law was that which influenced the lives of ordinary people most directly, and at least one historian considers that local self-government was real enough since 'early by-laws proceed from the farming community rather than from the lord of the manor'.[7] But any initiatives in this world are enjoyed by the yeomanry, not by the political and social elites of the 'county community'.

Such views blend with 'Country' perceptions of the corruptions of the Court expressed in the 'country house' poetry of Ben Jonson and Andrew Marvell and the classical pastoral of Milton. Whether they amount to a political philosophy in any positive sense is very doubtful indeed. The dominant view of the body politic was that expounded by Sir Thomas Wentworth in his speech to the Council of the North in December 1628. He stressed the 'joint individual well-being of sovereignty and subjection' and made no distinction between the local and central aspects of government. His insistence that 'distemper'd minds have of late very farr endeavoured to divide the consideracions of the two' was an attack on those who had allegedly confused 'private fortune' with the public good, not a comment on a wayward localism. His views were, at the level of political debate, unexceptionable. The historians who have written about the 'revolt of the provinces' have shown how conservative and how pragmatic the local response to the civil war was. This is not to deny the validity of the central/local split, or to wish away the civil war itself, but simply to argue for a lack of contemporary ideological basis for 'county' localism.

Proposals for the reform of local administration

Constitutional discussions and proposals from 1647 to 1649 touched upon local government, albeit indirectly as a consequence of the view that the centralised state should be dismantled. The army 'grandees' suggested in the Heads of the Proposals of August 1647 an element of popular election in the localities, although institutions were to remain unchanged. Justices of the peace were to be elected by grand jurors, themselves chosen in freeholders' meetings, and the King was to choose a sheriff from the three candidates nominated by the jurors of each county. The Levellers, particularly John Lilburne and Richard Overton, addressed the question more directly. They sought a complete reversal of the pattern of accountability by officials to superiors; election 'by the people in their respective places' was to be the new guiding rule. The parish was to be not only the basic unit of government but was to recover an administrative and political integrity which, according to the Levellers, it had lost at the Norman Conquest. There were to be courts in each hundred, consisting of elected jurors. All local officials were to be elected for a term of one year only. Tax assessors were to be elective. These plans amounted to 'a blue-print for a society of self-governing communities, with a large degree of voluntaryism'.[8] Dr Manning holds that the Levellers faltered and failed to press these proposals and that their uncertainty cost them political success, but the radicalism of their conception of local autonomy was an impediment in their campaign for acceptance of the Agreements of the People. Their views ran against an almost universal acceptance of authoritarian, paternalistic notions of government as the shared responsibility of governors and governed, of 'central' and 'local' authorities. The Levellers wanted more than 'devolution' or 'decentralisation'; they sought a flow of power from the parishes outwards which would leave the central authority at the furthest (and weakest) point of its scope.

The Levellers' idea of the primacy of each community percolated into later debates on law reform, as we shall discover, but their emphasis on political change was unique in exposing the injustice of how constitutional arrangements discriminated in favour of a wealthy and powerful oligarchy. Gerrard Winstanley perceived the fundamental injustice to be the ownership of property, and proposed in *The Law of Freedom in a Platform*, his most mature work, that issues of government would be settled by attention to the basis of relationships between individuals. There is an emphasis in Digger writings on the tasks of local governors, on their personal carriage, which is not to be found among the Levellers. Winstanley started from the premise that 'All . . . offices are like links of a chain, they arise from one and the same root, which is necessity of common peace', but apart from asserting the need for popular election of all officers, he offers no developed view of political democracy.

Those two most enduringly influential philosophers of the English Revolution, Hobbes and Harrington, have nothing of great moment to say about local government. Leviathan's power is indivisible, or at least there is to be allowed only such freedoms as he thinks fit. As Charles Blitzer points out, Harrington's *Oceana* leaves many responsibilities to local officials but he is surely mistaken to describe these as 'decentralisation'; Oceana's tax-collecting arrangements were those of early Stuart, 'centralised state', England.[9]

The Levellers were the only political thinkers of the English Revolution to devise a notion of 'local government' as the basis of political change. Their defeat in 1649 did not bury ideas of 'decentralisation', however: their standard passed to a group of radical lawyers, who as a pressure group in the Rump and in the Nominated Assembly came nearer to success than the Levellers had ever done, if success is to be judged in legislative achievement.

As both judicial and administrative tasks were the responsibility of local courts, law reformers can be viewed as local government reformers too, even though the burden of their demands emphasised codification of the criminal law. As in contemporary New England, 'law reform could not occur without a concomitant reformation of social institutions, economic conditions and political processes'.[10] And yet it seems that the radical lawyers thought it could, or thought at least that wider reform could be severely limited. The Leveller notion of county courts re-appears in the deliberations of the Hale Commission in 1652 and surfaced in a draft of a bill during Barebone's Parliament. The county judicatures would prevent 'unnecessary charge and delay in recovering of rights by the course of the common law'.[11] Mary Cotterell has argued that these courts were by no means independent of central control; they would have been outposts of the Courts of Common Pleas and the judges would not have been elected. Matthew Hale himself wanted to restore Common Pleas to primacy in civil cases against the unwelcome competition from King's Bench (or Upper Bench as it was during the 1650s). The Hale Commission is more evidence of a common lawyers' feud than of Leveller sympathies.

The lawyers confined themselves to procedural change, and did not propose extensive innovation in the common law itself. It is not surprising, however, that critics of the Hale Commission should have attributed to it more radical aims than those it actually espoused. After all, even if county judicatures were to be supervised from the centre, their very existence would have threatened the primacy of courts of quarter sessions in each county. Although they may best be considered as local branches of Common Pleas, the county courts would have dealt with 'all criminal matters' as well, and could have driven a wedge between the judicial and administrative powers of magistrates. Critics saw the dangers to the state and attacked notions of county autonomy:

> The interests of Rigths [sic] and Priviledges of each county . . . will protect malefactors and stop the whole Course of Justice; our own experience manifests the truth in the Courts of the Marches of Wales and the North . . . In each county the Judges will expound the Rule according to the several Interests in the Counties . . . so many Judicatories, so many several Laws.[12]

Here the argument of central *versus* local is laid bare; this is a rebuff to the Levellers as well as to the Hale Commission, and its tenor would have been echoed by Oliver Cromwell, enthusiast of legal reform though he was.

These sorts of proposals were consistently unpopular, if persistent in duration. They were usually associated with calls for county land registries. Henry VIII had intended these in the Statute of Enrolments of 1535 but the spirit if not the letter of the act had been flouted by common lawyers, who, to satisfy the demands of the propertied for secrecy in their transactions, had invented the collusive rigmaroles of fines and recoveries. Calls for land registries appeared in 1646 and later brought the business of the Rump to a standstill, appeared once more in 1653, again in the second Protectorate Parliament, in William Sheppard's

England's Balme of 1656 and in a curtain-call in 1659 in *Chaos, by a Well-Willer to the Common Weal.* Nothing concrete was achieved during the Interregnum, but some of the schemes, especially those of Barebone's Parliament, were worked out down to the details of office hours and the kind of ledger to be used. The argument for land registries was that 'every man may see what is his and what is another's'; the argument against was that they would unduly bolster the power of the state, whether centralised or 'cantonised':

> Thus may the State be intituled to most of the lands in England; hence also will the Commonwealth swarm with Informers, Prowlers and Searchers into others Titles.[13]

The interrelationship of central and local government

To summarise thus far: the consensus of opinion in mid-seventeenth-century England was that government was a matter of shared rights and obligations, to be interpreted by each subject according to his social position. There was no concept of boundaries between central and local responsibilities and no recognition that the rights of local governors could differ fundamentally from those of men in Whitehall (who were, in any case, also men of their own counties). The only concept of 'local government' which would have been acknowledged before the mid-1640s, before the appearance of county committees, would have been that of parish government and, in a more restricted sense, of manorial government, in which rights and obligations to the outside were minimal. Thus the advocacy by the Levellers of a reversed flow of obligations *was* strikingly original and it is not surprising that it stimulated other radicals and provoked opposition. The reforming lawyers seized on Leveller proposals for county judicatures and accommodated them into their own more cautious schemes for the reform of procedure; during the Interregnum change in local government structures was discussed only as an aspect of wider legal reform; there was no recognisable 'local government reform' lobby.

The Interregnum was, however, a legislatively fruitful decade and even if local institutions emerged largely unscathed at the end of it because there was no political will to alter them, it is worth looking for patterns which might emerge from the legislative achievement. Was it true that central control was slackened?

It must be recognised that acts of Parliament (and Protectoral ordinances) could be passed to satisfy local and specific interest groups, and that each statute should properly be examined in the light of pressure brought to bear on Westminster and Whitehall for and against it. The act against adultery and fornication, of 1650, and the Navigation Act of 1651 are considered by some to be the fruits of pressure-group politics; in the first case by Puritan ministers of the City of London, in the second by interloping free trade merchants. But those who would argue that it may not always be helpful to emphasise the stop- gap and the pragmatic in legislation may be succoured by Mr Thomas's proof that the 1650 act was the culmination of a century-long interest at Westminster in repression, and Mr Cooper's view that outside lobbying had nothing to do with the Navigation Act. There *is* a corpus of Interregnum legislation relating to local matters and it would be helpful to study it for any consistent trends or drifts, however inconsistent or ambivalent its origins and apparent purposes.

The principal organs of county government remained unaltered from the 1630s through to 1660, and indeed Lambarde's *Eirenarcha* of 1582 can be used with the Webbs' account of local government after 1688 to piece together the duties and avenues of responsibility. Sheriffs waited on the judges of assize, were held liable for certain crown, and later state, revenues and accounted to the Exchequer for them. Clerks of the peace were appointed by the *custos rotulorum*, who was *primus inter pares* of the bench of magistrates. The justices themselves were responsible to the Lord Keeper under the monarchy and during the Interregnum to parliament and subsequently to the Council of State. High constables were usually appointed at quarter sessions; petty constables in a bewilderingly wide variety of ways germane to their own parishes and manors.

THE SHERIFF

The Interregnum shrievalty exemplified the contradictions of 'settlement' and control, of how close to home governments had to fight a campaign of inducement and intimidation. Judge Francis Thorpe's charge to the assizes at York in March 1649 was, as charges always were, a propaganda exercise on behalf of the government, but it contained a profoundly conservative description of local obligations. Dearth had to be relieved by punishing middlemen, and weights and measures laws had to be enforced. The one passage in which Thorpe strayed from the Tudor/early Stuart orthodox, not to say commonplace, was in a discussion of the shrievalty:

> This is a great officer and is much trusted in the service of the people and by the state of *articulum super chartas*, is to be chosen yearly by the people, that they might the better be assured of those they trusted. But this privilege of election (among others) the people have lost and the court, of later times, did learn how to make profit, both by electing sheriffs, as also by keeping them off from being elected.[14]

The sheriff was the only elected official in Thorpe's catalogue; that in practice he was the most accountable to a department of government, the Exchequer, indicates the Judge's sanguine insistence on the popular basis of the Commonwealth: such a bold inversion of what was commonly observable suggests a degree of confidence by Thorpe which the later history of the Interregnum did nothing to justify. There was never any popular election of sheriffs and the difficulty encountered throughout the decade in finding reliable and willing men was partly a result of popular alienation, as well as a comment on the increasing burden of the office. In Warwickshire between 1647 and 1658 only four of the fourteen sheriffs were identifiable parliamentarians; in Glamorgan there were absentees; in other counties, including Kent, there were sheriffs who had been royalists.

The difficulties in securing a reliable shrievalty became critical during the interlude of the major-generals. The new militia, to act as a 'quick-sett hedge' for security, was to be paid for by the enemies of the state, and had to be supervised in each county by an official. The sheriff seemed the obvious choice. From November 1655 to January 1656 the major-generals tried to select suitable sheriffs from lists of two or three candidates sent to them by the Council of State. They immediately fell into the localist trap: the best man for the job should not be so badly treated as to be submitted to its expense. Major-General Berry cynically described the choice in one of the Welsh border countries:

> Mr Turvey is good for little; a rich clowne that would be glad to be taken notice of, and perhaps might be ruled. Mr Foley you all know,

> yet for his own sake I wish he might be spared, for the saying is here, that a man had as good be sequestered as made sherife.[15]

Even in more settled times, the office had been regarded as an onerous and (more importantly) expensive imposition. Much of the expense was incurred in entertaining judges and juries at assizes. J. S. Cockburn considers it 'obvious' that sheriffs 'were habitually open-handed at assize time'[16] but fails to square this with the resentment, the dread, which the call to office could invoke. More research would probably confirm that a generous scale of hospitality was institutionalised or built into the sheriff's duties. The other burden was that of supervising tax collection. Here the shrievalty had been discredited as the agency for ship-money; to be useful once more the office called for rehabilitation. An early act of the Rump allowed sheriffs their expenses in passing accounts but qualified this generosity in July 1650 by making sheriffs accountable for the distribution of all enacted legislation. (The easing of fees on owners of liberties the same year may appear as relief for those charged with collecting them, the sherriffs, but was really designed to make the purchase of confiscated lands more attractive.) Sheriffs were never reliable enough to be entrusted with the collection of the monthly assessments (which increased in Bedfordshire, for example, by over one-third between 1649 and 1652); they were left to receivers-general, usually soldiers, in each county.

The major-generals were left to correct the casual and inconsistent attitudes towards sheriffs of earlier governments of the 1650s. To excuse their friends from the office was to acknowledge that they were helpless. (After the major-generals had been voted down, it could be noted frankly in parliament that if the royalists were excluded from all offices, 'you will have neither sheriffs nor constables'.[17]) The major-generals chose instead to alter the pattern of appointments. In most of the counties of England and Wales there were only two or perhaps three appointments between 1655 and 1660 when there should have been five or six. Men acceptable to the government were found and then kept in office. These five years saw fewer appointments to the shrievalty than at any other time in the century. This despite the triumph of conservatism in central accounting procedures. Attempts to reduce the finances of the Commonwealth and Protectorate 'to one Treasury' had been frequent since the disbanding of the county committees in 1650. The victory of the Exchequer over the Treasury in 1654 has been viewed as evidence of the regime's conservatism, but the way in which the central court of the Exchequer and its old servants, the sheriffs, became separated suggests at least a spark of radicalism. The unity of the Exchequer, in London and in the counties, had been broken.

THE JURY

The shrievalty was thus an organ of local government which did receive legislative attention, unlike the commissions of the peace which were merely re-staffed as it became necessary. The jury system, too, was addressed directly. Briefly, juries, like justices, fulfilled an administrative as well as a judicial role. At assizes and quarter sessions they were to *present* offences, that is, to bring to the attention of the courts defects in roads and bridges, lapses in social obligations, both by communities and by individuals, as well as uncovered criminal offences. Schemes for the reform of juries centred on the compilation of accurate lists of freeholders so that no one of insufficient wealth or social standing could be impanelled. This task became more pressing in the aftermath of the civil wars; a jury of royalist sympathisers (or, after 1653, of Commonwealth sympathisers, not to mention Presbyterian partisans) could wreak havoc with official views of local justice, seen by most to be at the 'bowels' of the common weal. From the early 1650s, orders at quarter sessions were made for the listing of freeholders; a general order was sent to all the counties of the Western Circuit in 1648. In fact there had been complaints of 'insufficient' (ie inadequate in quality) juries from places as far apart as Devon and East Anglia as early as the 1610s, but in the 1640s and 1650s the problem was taken up by the radical lawyers and found a solution in one of the proposed Barebone's statutes. The orders do not seem to have borne fruit in the areas where they have been studied; as with the deficiencies in the shrievalty it was left to the major-generals to tackle the problems with any gusto. Possibly as a result of pressures brought to bear upon him by the Devon bench of magistrates, Oliver Cromwell wrote to the major-generals in January 1656. He spoke, characteristically, of the way in which the weak suffered at the hands of the 'subtle' who were insinuating themselves on to jury panels.[18] Here routine administration and his beloved 'reformation of manners' could meet.

Cromwell proposed the expedient of listing; the major-generals received the message each according to his own temperament. Disbrowe and Whalley were pessimistic; Worsley was, as ever, enthusiastic; Goffe asserted that this prosaic task of registration 'very much rejoyceth the people'.[19] Its effects were, as far as we can tell, as short-lived as the major-generals' campaign itself. Most historians seem agreed that the jury system was, in any case, a groundless worry; it displayed no independence and could easily be bullied into submission. It was simply an aspect of a general concern for security. The only flash of initiative among juries has been noted by J. S. Morrill in Cheshire; as well as frequently criticising the magistrates, the jury on a number of occasions nominated new justices. There are several peculiarities about administration in Cheshire, however. First, as a county palatine it was never visited by a circuit judge. Instead the county fell under the influence of John Bradshaw, who had presided at the trial of Charles I and who was Chief Justice of Chester. Secondly, the nominations and criticisms offered by the jury were all made at assizes, the court most directly under Bradshaw's control. Finally, there is evidence from a nearby Welsh county to support the view that Bradshaw manipulated the jury for his own purposes. In the summer of 1656, when the major-generals were campaigning to secure their sympathisers for the second Protectorate Parliament (and to exclude Bradshaw), the Flintshire jury suggested nine new men as justices. They were all moderate county gentry and the careers of two as Rump committeemen had coincided with Bradshaw's period as President of the Council of State. Bradshaw presided over the Court of Great Sessions in Wales and as the year 1656 was marked by his *contretemps* with Cromwell it seems more than coincidence that the Flintshire jury should suddenly erupt at the same time. The history of the institution both in Cheshire and in North Wales seems to prove simply that the jury was the property of whoever could control it.

The fortunes of trial by jury have been read as a measure of administrative radicalism during the civil war. Parliament relied heavily on the committee 'system' which bypassed the need for popular consent, and perhaps as significantly, obviated the need for extensive control. 'No ordinance between 1642–6 required the impannelling of juries.'[20] The 'middling sort' were denied their traditional voice in those years; should we regard the return to the jury in the legislation of the Protectorate as a belated victory of the freeholders? The new committees of 'judges' appointed to relieve 'poor prisoners' (debtors) under Barebone's was amended in 1654 to include a role for juries, but the emphasis during the 1650s was, as we have seen, on control; there is no evidence of any local initiatives to recover the rights of free juries, nor any enhancement of their duties in a new framework of local government.

THE CONSTABLE

At lower levels of local government participation, there were no significant changes in conditions or duties. There were increasing refusals by constables to take office but this was to be expected in a period of increasing central taxation. Not only were constables charged with the collection of the monthly assessment; after August 1649 they were called upon to collect the excise as well. There can be no doubt that the excise was an extremely unpopular tax, but its emergence should not be regarded as a simple act of centralisation. Certainly it was viewed by taxpayers as an unwarranted interference with 'liberties', but administrators of the excise were seen in different lights by different observers. Excisemen could be localists. One feature of the increased work-load of constables was that they could argue, in negotiations with their 'employers' at quarter sessions, that they were on the business of 'the state', as did the constables of Lancashire in 1652. But a general account of the office of constable must await future research; at present we are unable to distinguish overall patterns from the particular conditions of each county.

CENTRALISATION OR INTERFERENCE?

Those institutions directly tackled by central government were not the victims of 'centralisation', therefore, but were simply 'interfered with', in campaigns to secure the safety of the state as a whole, and to improve public finance. The 'centralisation' case is weakened still further if assizes and quarter sessions courts are considered. The former were used by the Commonwealth to secure consent to the political changes upon which it was founded, but assizes never again fulfilled the role of local government inspectorate which the early Stuarts had assigned to them. Assizes were inseparably associated with 'Thorough'. At quarter sessions 'angling for support' continued all through the Interregnum and changes in the commissions of the peace should not be taken as changes in the local power structure. Many were national changes only, especially those of the early 1650s.

Local performance in administration held up well during the Interregnum. No one now believes that poor relief collapsed during the decade because of some dour 'Puritan work ethic' which doomed the poor to self-help or starvation. Research on regions as diverse as Yorkshire, Cheshire, Warwickshire, Devon, Shropshire and London confirms that magistrates met their responsibilities squarely, if not always imaginatively. The pattern of relief varied considerably but the problem confronting local governors was one of money not of will. This could take several forms. In Devon it appeared as a series of imaginative orders at quarter sessions which, even after a torrent of vituperative attacks on defaulting accountants, ended in 1660 with virtually nothing accomplished. In London, finance was the greatest difficulty facing the governors of the new workhouse. By the later 1650s, these problems had produced new remedies. In Devon, Essex and Warwickshire there were moves towards the appointment of overall county treasurers, and in Cheshire a single county rate for all bridge repairs was planned. Unified county funding would have been hastened by an act of 1657 which stipulated that a separate rate for road repairs should be levied. It marked a shift away from labour towards fiscal obligations upon parishioners. In Hertfordshire the justices took over the funds of the disbanded militia bureaucracy for poor relief and other county purposes. There was a blurred image in the localities of a national drift away from fees towards salaries for officials, too.

It has been argued that there was no specific lobby for local government reform after the defeat of the Levellers, except where the plans of the radical lawyers for structural change touched upon it *en passant*. Changes were made *ad hoc*, and were a low priority except where they affected the physical and fiscal security of government. Interregnum legislation bore upon the conduct of everyday life in the provinces but it is remarkable how little of it—occupying 700 pages of *Acts and Ordinances of the Interregnum*—altered the procedures of local administration.

Central government agencies in the localities

If government enhanced its powers, its knowledge of local events, it did so not through the local courts but through central government agencies with outposts in the localities: the post office, the customs and excise offices, and, of course, the army and the establishments of the major-generals.

THE POST OFFICE

There was nothing new in governments trying to monitor the movement of population. Tudor statutes on alehouse control, for example, included injunctions to constables to inform magistrates of new arrivals in their parishes. Edmund Prideaux, postmaster-general from 1644 to 1653, developed the institution as an agency for government intelligence; Thomas Edwards, in *Gangraena*, indignantly chronicled outrages by the Independents in opening mail to and from London. Under the Rump this continued unchecked. From 1651 there were alternative schemes for farming the service; one was espoused by Thomas Pride and City of London radicals in an effort to oust Edmund Prideaux, no ally of theirs. The decision to farm was eventually taken under Barebone's.

Senior postal officers bitterly opposed the decision. In a reversal of the early Stuart pattern, in which members of parliament had volubly upheld the 'public good' against self-interested courtiers and monopolists, the officials argued that this parliamentary decision would allow private interests to prevail over public, and would forfeit the goodwill of the 'godly' (reliable) in the provinces. To scotch the scheme they even offered to guarantee a higher annual profit to the government, if necessary out of their own pockets, than the farmers were to return. They spoke for 'all the godly and well-affected postmasters'[21] and, as their own positions were not threatened, there is little reason to doubt them. After the Restoration the post office was considered to be a notorious refuge for adherents of the 'Good Old Cause'. So why farm? The timing of the decision, when radicalism was at a zenith in parliament, suggests a victory for the opponents of the conservative, Presbyterian Prideaux, and a radical government might be anxious to play down the significance of the office as an intelligence bureau. Certainly the legislation establishing the farm in September 1654 studiously avoided any reference to this side of the work. Preliminary instructions by the farmer, Captain John Manley, did include provisions for noting the names of travellers and guests at inns. These activities were to be kept secret, even though most people must have realised that postmasters had long been concerned in these matters. Even Gerrard Winstanley, of all people, thought that postmasters should inform governments of local events.

Manley's farm ran for an appointed two years but was not renewed. A committee chaired by Philip Jones, one of Cromwell's most trusted administrators, advised that the postal service should be 'farmed' to John Thurloe. This was a victory for the intelligence service. After the

Restoration one observer remembered that 'Another great intrigue of Cromwell was carefully to watch the Generall letter Office . . . for through this Office are conveyed all the poysonous distempers of the Citty into the whole Kingdome . . .'[22] Letters had been intercepted before, of course, but Cromwell employed one man, Isaac Dorislaus, to undertake this task. In an ordinance of June 1657, which strengthened government control over the post office, one of the functions of the office was declared to be 'to discover and prevent many dangerous and wicked designs which have been and are daily contrived against the Peace and Welfare of this Commonwealth'.[23]

One of the strengths of Interregnum governments was the quiet progress in home intelligence which enabled the plots of royalists and others to be nipped in the bud. The population was undoubtedly observed more closely but the enumeration of guests at inns was restrained, undertaken by postal officials who were self-effacing men about whom little is known. They were supported by local customs-house officers who, during the 1650s, were usually military men. 'Centralisation', if it means anything in this period, means the acquisition by government of a more finely tuned awareness of the behaviour of citizens.

THE REGISTRY

Postmasters were scrutinised by the major-generals in one of the highest priorities of their campaign, which began in the autumn of 1655. It was the aftermath of Penruddock's rising and at the heart of the instructions to the major-generals was a new means of observing the movement of population. In October a registry for the depositing of bonds taken from suspects was established. The procedures were elaborate and involved a double system of registration, to survey the movements of the disaffected *and* the innocent householder on the move. Secretary Thurloe was slow to execute the instructions of the Council as they touched upon the registry. In December Thomas Dunn was appointed as the registrar in London. His duties, office hours and even the number of ledgers he was to keep were all stipulated. By then the major-generals were inquiring, some rather tetchily, into the delays in introducing the scheme. Between January and April 1656 Dunn was hampered by his failure to secure suitable office accommodation in London, but he received no help from his employers. Despite these setbacks, Dunn sent out letters and printed forms to the major-generals on 1 January 1656 and soon the completed bonds began to return.

The registration plan has been attacked as 'too grandiose'[24] but it seemed to work adequately. The decimation tax, the meddling with juries and, above all, the lack of interested supervision from the centre provoked anguished outbursts from the major-generals; the taking of bonds, 'to which soe much of our work relates', went comparatively smoothly. The letter books and the volumes of suspects' names suggest efficiency not *folie de grandeur*. Of course there were problems, partly over Dunn's London address but chiefly in ensuring that travellers turned up at the office. Nevertheless, the system worked well enough to note the eighteen moves made by John Turner of Bletchingley in Surrey, the eleven journeys of Simon Heveningham of Richmond and the eight trips of Nicholas Borlase of Newlyn, Cornwall—all during 1656.

Disbrowe's sub-commissioners in Wiltshire, Dorset, Devon, Cornwall, Somerset and Gloucester took bonds from over 5,000 people. Their names were recorded, in alphabetical order, in one of Thomas Dunn's fat ledgers. The occupation or style of each was given, according to the instructions to the sub-commissioners by Disbrowe and Dunn. The lists were by no means simply a roll-call of ex-royalist delinquents. Rural tradesmen and county and parish gentry were all scrutinised, and if the homes of the Devon suspects are plotted on a map it appears that registration was most intense where the population was most concentrated, rather than where most of the royalists were. The registry worked in accordance with principles of administration, in other words, as well as with the political principles of its masters. Although the major-generals were voted down in Parliament on 28 January 1657, the registry continued to operate until April, and the last foreign suspect was registered on 10 August.

The major-generals' registry was apparently inspired by John Lambert, but the concept and scope of the institution echoed several earlier themes of the Interregnum. Comprehensive listing had been associated with jury control and with plans for land registries. The need for comprehensive information was being recognised, and, more importantly, seemed almost within the capacity of governments. The wider demands for security had been obvious in reforms in the post office and in the continued presence of the army. The major-generals and their registry were the civil and military aspects of security apotheosised together. The regulation of personal conduct, too, had a respectable pedigree before the men on horseback took up the challenge. Sexual offences, blasphemy, cock-fighting, race-meetings, swearing among dockers had all been attacked before 1655. What was new about the experiment was not its methods or its personnel but the principles behind it. It was a surrender to a hard-pressed minority in the counties who had borne 'the heat of the day'; it was an acknowledgment that their interests and those of others were not the same. The most enthusiasm for the scheme was evinced not by the major-generals themselves but by their subordinate commissioners in each county, who regarded themselves as a minority and who did not pretend to have public _____ n their side. They would have endorsed the sentim___ avalier, Sir John Gibson:

of my 'state
aluation;
a common fate
he Nation.[25]

1 ____ d indeed that of the other regimes
o ____ s of England and Wales has been
un ____ mething of parochial initiatives in
go ____ places the select vestry emerges from the
lat ____ ___s as a bulwark against anarchy in rural communities. Co ____ of 'ministers and the better sort' licensed alehouses in Che ____ e. The same 'middling sort' approval had to be found to obtain an alehouse licence in Exeter during the 1650s, and in the counties of Wiltshire, Worcestershire and Somerset. But at the same time there emerged, in some counties, in some parishes, a contrary symptom of enhanced power by magistrates. The campaign by Thomas Delavell, JP, in Houghton-le-Spring, County Durham, is an example. From the early 1650s Delavell supervised the activities of churchwardens and constables and annually scrutinised their accounts. Inspired by the publication of Henry Scobell's *A Collection of Acts and Ordinances*, in 1658, he wrote up the procedures to be followed by parish officials in their many aspects.

Elsewhere, there is evidence from the mid-1650s that magistrates were taking a greater interest in parish administration, evidence that cannot, for the most part, be related to the activities of the major-generals. There was an increasing spread of political participation which comprehended magistrates, churchwardens *and* major-generals' commissioners. Occasionally there *was* blatant interference, particularly in the boroughs before the elections to the second Protectorate Parliament. It could take the form of heavy-handed moral censure. Martin Pyke distributed fines taken from swearers and drunkards, to the poor of Hastings in 1656. Pyke was a Kentish man, so was both an outsider and a trespasser against local preferences for harmony not divisiveness. The weakening of determined reluctance to participate in government may be taken as a sign that a measure of political stability was returning under the Protectorate. By the 1670s parish vestries of the 'middling sort' *and* the petty sessions of the magistrates had both become unexceptional aspects of local government.

It was a lack of political support, either from the Protector or from parliament, which brought down the major-generals. But some have detected a lack of central enthusiasm for the scheme from its beginning, at least among civilian administrators like Thurloe. Cromwell himself was more interested in moral reformation than in the details of bureaucratic control. The episode of the major-generals certainly reveals the limitations of government, in the physical sense. Failures of communication were rife; difficulties over finance were a variation on this theme, as well. The major-generals and their registry were just an echo of committee government in the 1640s, in which there were no procedural rules, but simply a series of accretions, of *ad hoc* decisions accumulating to form their own frame of reference. The government was trying to operate on the frontiers of procedural possibility and it is difficult to see how it could have fared better. Thomas Dunn himself became a victim of bureaucratic inadequacy. After the registrar's office had been closed down he had had £200 *in toto* of his annual salary of £300. In June 1656 he had been owed £400; only half of that was found from militia funds. In October 1657 the Council of State was still ordering that Dunn should have £600 arrears of salary. His experiences matched exactly those of treasurers and governors of houses of correction in Devonshire; the same delays, the same need for persistent demands and the same desperate casting about for fiscal expedients.

Conclusions

Security and finance were the preoccupations of Interregnum legislators; no discernible pattern emerges beyond these themes. Laws controlling the maintenance of highways and establishing lay registrars of christenings, marriages and burials in each parish (another manifestation of a concern for numbers) seemed to widen the scope for participation by small freeholders. Small litigants, too, were helped by the abolition of fees which the filing of suits in Common Pleas had attracted. On the other hand, the vicious post-Restoration game laws were adumbrated in a statute of 1651 which not only allowed poachers to be convicted on oath before only one JP, but also provided cash rewards for informers, as in the 1620s. (Informing was also stimulated by 1650 legislation aimed at uncovering concealed delinquents' estates.) The protection of property is a common, if tenuous thread here; the governments of the Interregnum were, in this respect, unexceptional.

The 'centralisation' which occurred during the 1650s was of a very specific kind. It did not develop through institutional change. The decline of the assize circuits as an agency of control by far outweighed in significance the temporary monitoring of juries and population. Here, control developed in one case as a practicable aspect of legal reform and in the other as a simple matter of state security. In neither case did change improve the performance of the tasks of government in the localities. There was no shift in the pattern of decision- making from local to central levels. If 'interference' is substituted for 'centralisation', if the major-generals are seen simply as meddlers rather than as agents of the centralising state, our understanding is improved. But when historians have spoken of 'centralisation' they have meant the presence of soldiers in the counties as commissioners for assessments and for ejecting scandalous ministers. Their existence does not outweigh the drift from interference. The 'collapse' of central government interest in local government in 1660 is an illusion which the presence of the men on horseback has created among historians. Rather than centralisation in the 1650s, succeeded by a revulsion from this at the Restoration (and here interpretations of 'government' have followed the perceived fortunes of 'Puritanism'), there was probably a shift in the relationship between Whitehall and the provinces which developed steadily from the remedial legislation of 1641. Seen in this light, the major-generals appear as temporary successors to the assize judges and to the apparatus of conciliar control.

Notes

1. E. M. Leonard, *The Early History of English Poor Relief* (Cambridge, 1900), p. 156.
2. T. B. Macaulay, *The History of England from the Accession of James II*, ed. T. F. Henderson, 5 vols (Oxford, 1931), Vol. i, p. 120.
3. D. Underdown, 'Settlement in the Counties', in G. E. Aylmer (ed.), *The Interregnum* (London, 1972), p. 166.
4. H. Simon, *Administrative Behaviour* (New York, 1957), p. 38.
5. Ivan Roots, 'Cromwell's Ordinances', in Aylmer (ed.), *The Interregnum*, p. 212.
6. John Norden, quoted in Eric Kerridge, *Agrarian Problems in the Sixteenth Century and After* (London, 1969), p. 31.
7. W. O. Ault, 'Some Early Village Bylaws', *English Historical Review*, 45 (1930), p. 231.
8. Brian Manning, *The English People and the English Revolution* (London, 1976), p. 328.
9. Charles Blitzer, *An Immortal Commonwealth: The Political Thought of James Harrington* (New Haven, 1960), p. 259.
10. G. L. Haskins, *Law and Authority in Early Masachusetts* (New York, 1960), p. 687.
11. 'Several Draughts of Acts . . .', in W. Scott (ed.), *Somers Tracts*, 13 vols (1809–15), Vol. vi, p. 211.
12. *Reasons Against the Bill Entituled An Act for County Registers* (1653), p. 20.
13. 'Several Draughts of Acts'; *Reasons Against the Bill*, p. 7.
14. 'Sergeant Thorpe's Charge', in W. Oldys (ed.), *Harleian Miscellany*, 8 vols (1744–6), Vol. ii, p. 11.
15. T. Birch (ed.), *State Papers of John Thurloe*, 7 vols (1742), Vol. iv, p. 215.
16. J. S. Cockburn, *A History of English Assizes 1558–1714* (Cambridge, 1972), pp. 104–5.
17. J. T. Rutt (ed.), *Diary of Thomas Burton*, 4 vols (1828), Vol. ii, p. 34.
18. W. C. Abbott, *The Writings and Speeches of Oliver Cromwell*, 4 vols (Cambridge, Mass, 1937–47), Vol. iv, pp. 87–8.
19. Birch, *Thurloe State Papers*, Vol. iv, p. 639.
20. J. S. Morrill, *The Revolt of the Provinces* (London, 1974), p. 77.
21. British Library Add. Ms. 22, 546 f 123.
22. C. H. Firth, 'Thurloe and the Post Office', *English Historical Review*, 13 (1898), pp. 527–33.
23. C. H. Firth and R. S. Rait (eds), *Acts and Ordinances of the Interregnum*, 3 vols (London 1911), Vol. ii, pp. 1110–13.

24. Anthony Fletcher, *A County Community in Peace and War: Sussex 1600–1660* (London, 1975), p. 304.

25. *North Country Diaries*, 2nd series (Surtees Society, 124, 1915), p. 52.

4

Oliver Cromwell and his Protectorate Parliaments: Co-operation, Conflict and Control*

Peter Gaunt

It is now nearly forty years since the publication of Trevor-Roper's seminal article on Oliver Cromwell and his parliaments. It portrayed Cromwell as an idealistic but incompetent parliamentarian, an industrious back-bencher, ill-equipped to deal with the legislature when elevated to senior military and political office. From the late 1640s until his death, Cromwell faced a succession of assemblies which he failed to understand, work with or manage, standing by bewildered and generally inactive as other ably-led cliques seized the initiative and promoted deliberately destructive and antagonistic policies. For Trevor-Roper, Cromwell's relations with parliaments, particularly those of the Protectorate, comprised a series of abject failures and unconstitutional

*This article is in part based upon a paper presented, in slightly different versions, to an early modern Britain conference held in Wellington, New Zealand, in 1985, and to the seventeenth century seminar group at the Institute of Historical Research in 1989; I am grateful to all who attended for their comments and suggestions. An article springing from part of that paper, entitled 'Law-Making in the First Protectorate Parliament' appeared in C. Jones, M. Newitt and S. Roberts (eds), *Politics and People in Revolutionary England* (Oxford, 1986). Inevitably, some points made and material used in that article reappear here, though I have tried to keep such repetition to a minimum.

counter-attacks, born of his inability to win parliament's co-operation, impose his wishes upon the legislature or adopt the techniques by which his Tudor and Stuart predecessors had managed their unruly parliaments.[1] The article tends to confirm, albeit in more measured and academic tones, a view which surfaced during Cromwell's own lifetime and which has outlived him for more than three centuries—Cromwell the inveterate enemy of representative assemblies, whose uneasy relations with parliament reached breaking point as the two struggled for control of the post-regicide ship of state. To many of his contemporaries, Cromwell was a devious schemer, a Machiavelli or a Borgia, who had been quietly plotting his own advance to the helm since the mid-1640s, if not earlier, and who achieved his goal of absolute despotism during the 1650s. Opposition literature published during the Protectorate and immediately before and after the Restoration portrays a tyrannical Oliver who looked upon parliament with suspicion and who saw it as, at best, an irrelevant distraction and, at worst, a dangerous obstacle and rival. Accordingly, he manipulated, disregarded or ruthlessly destroyed successive assemblies. The rights and liberties of the people in parliament were trampled underfoot and extinguished.[2]

Shorn of their royalist or republican excesses, these bleak contemporary images of Cromwell and his treatment of parliament have proved remarkably durable. In his supposed subversion of representative assemblies, the Protector has over the years been likened to a whole host of unsavoury characters, from Caesar and Napoleon to Hitler and Mussolini. In 1894–5 English as well as Irish MPs and peers reacted with horror to Lord Rosebery's proposal to erect a statue of this enemy of parliament within the Palace of Westminster. Neither Lords nor Commons wanted a likeness of Cromwell within their lobbies and corridors and the statue was eventually placed outside, in the Palace precincts. Parliament had refused to pay for the work and Rosebery met the costs out of his own pocket, anonymously. In 1902 Huntingdon's MP, G. C. Montagu, led similar and successful opposition to plans to erect a statue of Cromwell in the town of his birth. In such manner has the contemporary portrayal of Cromwell—that of the champion of the parliamentary cause turned inveterate, embittered enemy of parliaments —been accepted and repeated by successive generations, including our own. Many historians still view the Cromwell of the 1650s as a bigger threat to parliament than Charles I had ever been. Even Trevor-Roper, in the most detailed and in some ways sympathetic modern assessment published on the subject, sees Cromwell's relations with his parliaments as, at heart, a sorry and sordid tale of force and fraud, purges, expulsions and recriminations.

Yet as Trevor-Roper himself points out, Cromwell never came to oppose parliaments in principle and for all the difficulties and the dubious expedients which followed, it is quite wrong to see the Protector as an implacable enemy of parliament, setting out wilfully to undermine or dispense with them. The very opposite. Although it is often impossible to fathom Cromwell's political views—indeed, he probably held to no coherent or consistent political philosophy during the civil war and Interregnum[3]—a representative body of some kind seems to have remained a crucial component of all his plans and aspirations throughout the period. The powers and duration of parliament may have to be limited, security may necessitate restrictions upon those entitled to elect or be elected, but representatives should continue to meet and transact business.

The Protector's links with parliament were close. He sat in three parliaments and spent around fourteen years, almost a quarter of his entire life, as an MP. During the 1650s, with a standing army of nearly 60,000 at his command, Cromwell might have been able to dispense with parliaments and rule by the sword and military edict, at least for a time. In reality, he attempted no such thing and, as far as we know, never even toyed with the idea.[4] Even when parliament after parliament went astray, his faith in the institution apparently survived unshaken. From July 1653 to January 1658 he summoned three assemblies and opened four sessions, greeting each with a fulsome speech loaded with a joy and optimism which were surely unfeigned if also sadly misplaced. In September 1654, for example, MPs were treated to a discourse on the achievements of the newly established government, culminating in this magnificent occasion. It was, Cromwell declared, 'the hopefullest day that ever mine eyes saw, as to the considerations of this world'. 'To have such a day of hope as this is, and such a door of hope opened by God to us, truly, I believe, some months since would have been beyond all our thoughts.' The parliament, Cromwell had no doubt, would lay the topstone to the new government and bring the ship of state into a safe harbour. The glory would accrue to this sweet and gracious assembly.[5] With the benefit of hindsight, it is these welcoming speeches, sometimes almost messianic in tone, which appear particularly tragi-comic. The failure of one assembly seems not to have seriously diminished his high

hopes as the next assembled. True, in 1656 Cromwell initially contemplated a non-parliamentary way to fill the empty coffers, but, having
heard the arguments of his councillors and the major-generals, he decided
to summon another parliament and he duly welcomed the MPs with
unblunted optimism.[6] Undaunted by the chaotic end of the second
Protectorate Parliament, Cromwell was laying plans for a third during
the last months of his life.[7]

Cromwell's role in the Long Parliament has been traced through the
1640s in a number of works, culminating in Underdown's masterly
treatment of the political and military circumstances surrounding
Pride's Purge.[8] The Lord General's influence inside and outside the
Rump is analysed in detail by Worden.[9] Woolrych has continued
the story up to December 1653, tracing the birth, life and induced suicide
of the Nominated Assembly, 'my poor little invention' as Cromwell
later called it.[10] But for the two Protectorate parliaments we possess
no full-length published accounts. The main events of the sessions
can be followed in general narratives of the period, the best and fullest
that of Gardiner up to summer 1656, continued by Firth through to
Cromwell's death.[11] Brief articles have explored certain aspects of the
two parliaments—Gaunt on exclusions from and law-making within
the first Protectorate Parliament, Roots on law-making in the second,
Wilson and Merli on the Naylor case, Firth and others on the kingship
controversy.[12] A handful of American and British theses have also been
undertaken, some good, some indifferent; the best, by Sarah Jones,
certainly deserves publication.[13] But a comprehensive and compelling
full-length account of these parliaments is badly needed. The appearance
of the relevant *History of Parliament* volumes on these parliaments,
currently in preparation, will help clarify certain issues via biographical
analysis of the MPs but will by no means fill the yawning gap. Thus
nearly forty years on, the most forceful analysis of Cromwell's relations
with his two Protectoral parliaments remains the relevant sections
of Trevor-Roper's wide-ranging article 'Oliver Cromwell and his
Parliaments', which first appeared in the mid-1950s. In a brief but
pertinent article published in 1988, Roger Howell questioned some of
Trevor-Roper's assumptions and interpretations, though he did not go
on to expound and expand on an alternative interpretation of his own.[14]
Much more could be said both in response to the Trevor-Roper thesis
and in an attempt to lay out a different picture of Cromwell's relations
with his two Protectorate parliaments. Such comments as space allows

here may be grouped under three headings: co-operation, conflict and control.

The first Protectorate Parliament assembled on 3 September 1654, Cromwell's lucky day, the anniversary of his victories at Dunbar and Worcester. It sat for twenty weeks, the minimum allowed under the constitution, and was dissolved by Cromwell in January 1655. The second Protectorate Parliament, an additional parliament called before the next regular triennial assembly was due, met on 17 September 1656 and remained in session for nine months, working through Christmas and Easter, until the House rose in late June 1657. Members reassembled in January 1658 for what turned out to be a very brief and stormy second session, ended by dissolution within a fortnight. Thus parliament was in session for a little under fifteen of the fifty-seven months of Oliver Cromwell's Protectorate.

They were quite extraordinary assemblies, like no others before or since. They met under the terms of a written constitution, a constitution which defined the role of the legislature within the Protectoral regime and contained specific provisions governing the frequency, duration, composition and powers of parliament. In the process, the constitution laid out a number of novel provisions, redefining the franchise and drastically redistributing the seats, setting tests and examinations for would-be members, limiting parliament's legislative rights and specifying certain legislative procedures. But parliament was also ascribed carefully defined and quite extensive powers to examine and supervise the actions of the executive. The House of Commons was made up of 460 elected members, representing not only England and Wales but also Ireland and Scotland, thus achieving parliamentary union of sorts. The revised constitution of summer 1657 provided for a second non-elected chamber, broadly along the lines of the old House of Lords, but for all except the fortnight-long session of January and February 1658, Oliver Cromwell's two Protectorate parliaments comprised a House of Commons alone.[15]

The written constitutions apparently gave parliament very wide and supreme legislative power, together with sweeping rights to oversee and control the actions of the executive, principally a single head of state assisted by a permanent Council. However, even on paper there were distinct limitations to parliament's powers, for under the terms of the Instrument of Government it need be in session for just five in any thirty-six months and could be dissolved at any time once the guaranteed minimum period had elapsed, large areas of policy, including the religious and financial settlements enshrined within the written constitution of December 1653 and, in theory at least, the whole constitution itself, were deemed inviolable and beyond alteration by parliament, and any legislation could be vetoed by the Protector without question or appeal on the grounds that it ran counter to the Instrument. Yet the written constitutions genuinely attempted to encourage contact and co-operation between executive and legislature and to ensure a smooth working relationship. Parliament relied upon the executive to approve and implement legislation but could be held in check by veto and dissolution. The executive looked to parliament to approve and confirm policies and appointments made during the intervals between sessions and to grant supplementary funds in times of need. There was considerable overlap of personnel, as many government officials, including councillors, won election to the House. Above all, the two arms of government were united by the Lord Protector, for in addition to his role as head of state and of the executive, the Protector was vested with joint legislative power. Article I of the Instrument declared that 'supreme legislative authority' resided in 'one person, and the people assembled in parliament'. Protectoral assent was necessary before a parliamentary bill could become law. Under the terms of the written constitutions, for the legislature and the executive to work effectively and to the full, it was necessary that they work together. How far was such co- operation achieved in practice?

The MPs spent much of their time discussing the very highest matters of state, for both parliaments were dominated by constitutional reform. The Instrument of Government was brought into question on the first working day of the 1654 parliament and was debated at almost every sitting thereafter; MPs were still working on the Government Bill when Cromwell summoned them to the Painted Chamber to be dismissed. The constitution rarely came to the fore during the opening months of the second Protectorate Parliament, but from February to June 1657 MPs were absorbed in the drafting and passage of the Humble and Additional Petitions. The operation of this new constitution provoked the disagreements and confrontations which wrecked the second session and led to the hasty dissolution. Thus both parliaments were heavily involved in constitutional revision and redrafting. Every facet of government was examined in the course of these debates, some in meticulous detail, some with great heat. Should the state be headed by a single person and, if so, what title and powers should he possess? Was a second chamber needed and what should be its role? Who was to have control over the army, the direction of foreign policy, the declaration of war and peace, the appointment of senior military, civilian and judicial officers, the imposition, collection and use of the state finances, and so on? In short, parliament discussed and ordered every aspect of the central direction of the state, up to and including the very foundations and fundamentals of government. MPs calmly—sometimes not so calmly—discussed who or what should govern Britain and in what manner. Rarely, if ever, had St Stephen's Chapel witnessed such debates.

Yet it was not all high politics, and MPs did not spend the whole session locked in major political conflicts or battling through a jungle of constitutional reform. There is a side to these parliaments far removed from Trevor-Roper's story of constitutional conflict and failure, a side almost entirely ignored and implicitly denied by him. There is far more to these parliaments than the sorry tale of executive trickery and mismanagement, of confrontations over Naylor and the major-generals and set-piece battles over the constitution, which form the staple fare of most histories of the period. Even Gardiner and Firth rarely progress far beyond this grisly tale. There is a very different side to these parliaments, a picture of MPs working in something approaching harmony with their fellow members and with the Protector, handling a mass of business and meeting some of the requirements (principally financial) for which they had been summoned. More than this, it is a picture of the Protectoral MPs fulfilling what might be called the traditional role of a seventeenth-century parliament, that of the grand court of the nation, a forum for discussing and advising on questions of the moment, for hearing appeals, receiving petitions and redressing a wide range of grievances. In dealing with a mass of routine and local business, MPs sought to aid their friends, family and constituents, and to promote the interests of their own localities. This picture of Protectoral parliaments peacefully conducting the customary business of an early modern parliament in the customary ways contrasts not only with Trevor-Roper's image of rootless and unmanageable assemblies wildly adrift in a sea of constitutional destruction, but also with the portrayal of Protector and parliament as inveterate antagonists.

In his brief but excellent article on law-making in the second Protectorate Parliament, Ivan Roots has already drawn attention to the constructive side of the 1656–7 session. Certainly there were periods of confrontation, with angry outbursts and destructive disunity over certain issues—exclusions at the start of the session, the Naylor case in December, some aspects of the constitution, principally kingship, the following spring. But much of the Humble Petition was accepted with few histrionics and overall we have a picture of a reasonably harmonious and productive session. Sixty acts reached the statute books, quite a respectable total for a forty-week session. They included public statutes of national and political importance: annulling the pretended title of Charles Stuart, defining treason, confirming the abolition of purveyance and of the court of wards and liveries, imposing the monthly assessments and setting excise rates. Others reflected social, economic and religious interests common to all early modern English parliaments, not merely those of the so-called Puritan Revolution: an act against vagrants and wandering, idle, dissolute persons, an act for the better observation of the Lord's Day, an act for punishing such persons as live at high rates and have no estate, profession or calling answerable thereunto, an act for discovering, convicting and suppressing of Popish recusants, acts dealing with the production, sale, import or export of wine, corn and other foodstuffs, an act on fishing and so forth. But many of the acts which passed in 1656–7 reflected local or private interests: the preservation of woods and timber in Gloucestershire, the settlement of Gloucester cathedral upon the mayor and burgesses of the city for religious and charitable uses, the indemnification or reward of named individuals, the establishment of ministers in Plymouth, Exeter, Bristol, Great Yarmouth, Northampton and Newport, Isle of Wight.

Over one hundred other bills were introduced and considered during the session, but fell by the wayside for some reason; many were incomplete when the House rose in June and were lost when the unproductive second session was abruptly ended. Thus legislation on land draining in Hampshire and Essex, the transport of food in and around Norwich, the repair of Ely cathedral, maltmaking, the care of orphans, bastardy, alehouses, wrecks, wages, holy days and a myriad of other topics would have to await another parliament. MPs were almost overwhelmed by the flood of petitions relating private or local grievances and from time to time made half-hearted resolutions to receive no more for a week, or to transact no private business for a fortnight. In practice, the steady flow of petitions was rarely disrupted and, even during the opening months of 1657 when the session was dominated by long debates over the major-generals, kingship and the new constitution, public and private bills continued to be considered, slotted in early in the morning or whenever MPs found an hour or two—sometimes just a few minutes—to spare.[16]

So much for the second Protectorate Parliament. But what of the first? What absorbed MPs during the twenty-week session of 1654–5? Carlyle was emphatic, magisterial and unremittingly condemnatory:

> A most poor hidebound Pedant Parliament; which reckoned itself careful of the Liberties of England; and was careful only of the Sheepskin Formulas of these; very blind to the Realities of these! Regardless of the facts and clamorous necessities of the Present.[17]

Indeed, this parliament seems to fit more closely Trevor-Roper's image —rather restrained in comparison to Carlyle's—of unrelieved and unmanaged chaos. Certainly, the draft constitution was considered almost daily throughout the session, provoked many fierce engagements and led to an angry dissolution at the earliest opportunity and before any legislation, from the Government Bill downwards, had reached the statute book. Yet even the limited sources which survive—chiefly the Commons Journal and Guibbon Goddard's sparse and incomplete diary—reveal that amidst this apparent cauldron of political strife and failure, MPs found time to engage in more customary and less frenetic parliamentary business. Over forty bills were introduced during the session and several, including the assessment bills for England, Scotland and Ireland and a bill against the court of wards, were all but complete at the dissolution. There was legislation on chancery and treason, probate of wills, the unifying of England and Ireland, the ejection of scandalous ministers, printing, marriage, Quakers, drunkards, idiots and lunatics. Bills were introduced to encourage the restoration of cathedrals, to relieve poor prisoners at York, to establish law courts in the four northern counties, to restrict the transport of geldings and to promote the management of salt petre.

Despite several temporary embargoes on the receipt of petitions, a mass of local and private grievances also came before the House. Bills were initiated to settle lands on the heirs of Samuel Dingley and William Masham, deceased, and to naturalise a number of aliens long resident in England. The Earl of Worcester was granted his freedom on bail, the Earl of Clanrichard given leave to stay in England for six months. MPs referred rival petitions from Lord Craven and Sir John Stowell over disputed property rights to a parliamentary committee, unwittingly stirring up a hornet's nest involving a host of titled witnesses, testimony from Protectoral councillors and a number of printed expositions. The people of Surrey complained that their sheriff had quietly pocketed £1,200 raised out of local assessments to pay for a common gaol and house of correction within the county; a committee examined the case and introduced a bill to compel the errant sheriff to disgorge the money. A petition regarding the 'late disappointment' of the Greenland fleet and the consequent shortage of oil prompted MPs to examine the conduct of the whaling companies and the supply of oil; someone mentioned the similar shortage of corn and the debate quickly widened into a general review of the nation's trade which lasted all morning and ended with a resolution—poorly observed, as it turned out—that a Committee of the Whole on Trade should meet once a week. Thus the main business of the day, consideration of one of the most important issues in the draft constitution, namely whether the Protectorship should be elective or hereditary, was jostled out by whale oil and corn carriers. It is all a long way from the traditional story of unbroken political intrigue and constitutional infighting, from Carlyle's parliament of hidebound MPs who cared only for 'the painful new modelling of the government and were blind to the clamorous necessities of the people'.[18]

It would, however, be patently absurd to project Cromwell and his parliaments in this light alone. There was, clearly, a disruptive and turbulent side to these assemblies, a side which provoked tests and exclusions, disunity and division and, ultimately, angry and abrupt dissolution. What, then, were Cromwell's aspirations of his two Pro-tectorate parliaments and how and why did they fall short of these aspirations?

Cromwell's own views of his relationship with parliament are revealed in the course of his opening speeches to his two Protectorate parliaments. The speeches were loaded with expressions of a profound reverence and respect for the institution. He saw parliament as ' blessing', a source of liberty and hope and the font of 'mercy, truth, righteousness and peace'. It was also to be the vehicle for perfecting and securing the new order and an impregnable bulwark against any threats to the regime. The legislature was held to be the very embodiment of the three nations, their people and the divinely sanctioned beliefs for which they had sacrificed so much, and its members therefore had a duty to protect, defend and serve the Godly cause: 'to promote the glory of God against the Common Enemy, to suppress everything that is Evil, and encourage whatsoever is of Godliness'. In short, Cromwell saw parliament as a vital element of the new regime and expected it to play an active and important role within the state, carrying onerous responsibilities and sharing the heavy load of government. He repeatedly stressed that the written constitution obliged Protector and parliament to act together in discharging legislative and other duties and he claimed that he had accepted office only in the belief that sympathetic parliaments would work with him in the pursuit of these common goals. He saw the relationship as one based upon close collaboration and co-operation and viewed Protector and parliament as partners in government. Accordingly, he proclaimed that he would neither obstruct members nor impose his will from above and that his parliaments were truly 'free', a freedom 'which, as I have desired above my life, I shall desire to keep it so above my life'. In September 1654 he half apologised for lecturing MPs upon the problems of government, telling them that 'I have not spoken these things as one that assumes to himself dominion over you, but as one that doth resolve to be a fellow-servant with you, to the interest of these great affairs and of the people of these nations'. 'I shall be ready to stand and fall with you', he told his second Protectorate Parliament. He looked for a 'union' and 'love' between Protector and parliament, on occasion carrying the imagery of intimacy to its natural conclusion: 'I should be very glad to lay my bones with yours . . . with all heartiness and cheerfulness'.[19]

Yet this cheerful partnership was soon shown to be far from equal and MPs discovered that the much-vaunted parliamentary freedom had distinct limits. Cromwell viewed himself as the ultimate arbiter, 'being set on a watch-tower to see what may be for the good of these Nations', and possessed of a duty to intervene if parliament deviated from the desired path. That path was defined with varying clarity as due observance of the Protector's position and other fundamental tenets of the constitution, the promotion of godly reformation and broad liberty of conscience, the safeguarding of the three nations and their government at home and abroad and, most hazily of all, non-interference in the affairs of the army. All other business was a matter for consultation between and amendment by Protector and parliament, and Cromwell declared himself open to approaches and persuasion from the House 'towards mutual conviction'. But the vital elements of the existing settlement, 'the fruits of our blood and travail', were not negotiable and could not be abandoned at any cost—'I can sooner be willing to be rolled into my grave, and buried with infamy'—and parliament would not be allowed to undermine them. Cromwell believed that he had 'a duty to God and the people of these nations, to their safety and good in every respect', which was superior to and if necessary overrode his duty to parliament. 'Necessity hath no law', Cromwell told his parliament, and he made it very clear by both his words and his actions that whenever he alone judged parliament to be threatening the godly cause, he would intervene with whatever force was necessary—persuasions and threats, tests and purges, veto or dissolution—to prevent 'the wilful throwings away of this government' by the legislature.[20]

The Protector had expansive but rather imprecise expectations of his two Protectoral parliaments. It becomes apparent, both from the Protector's opening speeches and from subsequent events, that Cromwell had no clear plans for the session, no detailed and comprehensive list of objectives which had to be fulfilled. The speeches at the opening of parliament, grand, often eloquent, sometimes moving, were also remarkably thin on specifics. Acutely aware of the insecurity of the regime and the threats to the godly cause from all sides, Cromwell made it clear in his opening speeches that he had summoned parliament to observe, preserve and strengthen the existing settlement and to maintain and develop policies already in train towards these ends. Thus parliament was expected to confirm the work of Protector and Council, including their ordinances of 1653–4 and the Spanish war begun in 1655–6, to provide cash needed to continue the struggle against enemies at home and abroad, and to pursue with renewed vigour existing Protectoral policies aimed at securing the nation and reforming the moral and personal welfare of its people. Such ends could best be met by legislation and although Cromwell occasionally voiced a criticism common at the time, that the statute book was already overloaded and that government should reduce, not expand, the body of law, he none the less expected MPs to promote parliamentary bills. He roundly condemned his first Protectorate Parliament for its failure to complete any legislation—'to make those good and wholesome laws which the people expected from you'—and praised the second for its diligence in presenting so many bills for his approval, while urging it on to prepare more 'that tend to reformation, to the discountenancing of vice, [and] to the encouragement of good men and virtue'. Above all, however, Cromwell wanted a secure governmental base and, in the wake of so much constitutional change and instability, he was anxious that the legislature should approve and guarantee firm and permanent foundations for his regime. Initial expectations that MPs would quickly and almost unquestioningly confirm *in toto* the Instrument of December 1653 were soon dispelled and he acknowledged parliament's right to reform the constitution, provided certain fundamental provisions were retained. In the event, the 1654–5 Government Bill did not provide the durable, effective and widely acceptable platform which he sought. By 1656 Cromwell more readily appreciated that the Instrument was defective and he welcomed its revision in parliament. Kingship apart, he accepted the Humble and Additional Petitions unreservedly as a new beginning and a stable, long-term foundation for his government.

Despite his hopes for the sessions, Cromwell did not use his speeches at the opening of parliament to provide a tangible lead, still less to lay out specific proposals. In September 1654 most of the opening speech comprised a review of government over the preceding nine months, showing how chaos had been turned to peace, stability and internal unity. The ship of state had been steered to calmer waters and parliament had merely to continue the course already set to reach the safe harbour. In 1656 the circumstances were very different and the House was called upon, not to put the top stone to the glorious edifice, but to counter great dangers and save the godly cause from imminent overthrow. Accordingly, Cromwell's opening speech concentrated on these threats at home and abroad, defending the Spanish war and the major-generals. In 1654 he had wanted parliament to complete the process of 'healing and settling'; two years later the watchwords were 'security' and 'reformation'. But in 1654 and 1656 alike, the Protector spoke in general terms about the general situation and made few concrete proposals for the coming session.

Explicit requests of parliament tended to be listed quite briefly near the end of the speeches, almost as an unimportant addendum to the principal business. The requests, for further reformation, alliances with friendly powers, the vigorous pursuit of enemies at home and abroad and the supply of much-needed money, were wide-ranging but vague. For example, in 1656 Cromwell made 'reformation' one of the sub-headings of his speech and repeatedly referred to the need for moral reform, but when he finally broached the subject, his comments were vague, general and covered in a single paragraph. There was much 'profaneness, disorder and wickedness in all places', he told MPs, and they had a duty to root it out, casting down sin and sinners and elevating purity. But there were no detailed or concrete suggestions, no proposals that the House consider specific issues—alehouses, bastardy, vagrancy, gaming or whatever—and MPs were merely pointed in the general direction. Although many such topics were covered by subsequent legislation, it was generally initiated by unplanned and *ad hoc* occurrences, rather than by the introduction into the House of an already prepared legislative programme by Cromwell's agents. Again, it is noticeable that of the three main issues of the 1656–7 session—the Naylor case, the Militia Bill and new constitution—all seem to have come to the fore in unplanned and unexpected ways, none had been presaged by Cromwell's opening speech and none were introduced by Protectoral agents and presented as the wishes of Protector and executive.[21]

It is clear that the executive had not worked out a programme of essential public legislation prior to the session. True, in his opening speech of September 1654, Cromwell told the first Protectorate Parliament that bills to reform the legal system were in preparation and 'in due time I make no question will be tendered unto you'. In practice, such legislation on the subject as was considered during the subsequent session was drafted in committee, not introduced ready made by Cromwell's friends, agents or councillors. Some apparently sprang from unplanned or unforeseen events, such as the receipt of petitions from particular individuals or groups, and others had their origins in attacks upon or faults within some of the conciliar ordinances of 1653–4. The opening months of the second Protectorate Parliament were calm and rather empty—Thurloe caught the mood perfectly when he wrote in early December 1656 'we still jogg on in the parliament without doing anything very extraordinary'.[22] Councillor MPs and others had ample time and opportunity to introduce a governmental legislative programme. But the 'courtiers', as the parliamentary diarists sometimes term them, had no programme in hand and instead from late September MPs were left to prepare their own legislation in line with the hazy pointers of the Protector's opening speech, the needs of themselves, their constituency and their constituents, and any other ideas and initiatives which came to hand. Not surprisingly, MPs drifted along with a mass of worthy, very varied and largely unexciting legislation, much of it springing from *ad hoc*, unplanned roots. Cromwell seemingly did not feel that it was his right or duty, either in the opening speech or subsequently through the activities of councillor MPs or other agents in the House, to set forth a detailed programme of business or a comprehensive legislative programme. He seems to have believed that the

MPs would share his appreciation of the current situation and, with God to guide them, would respond by working together to fulfil the general needs and aspirations of the nation as laid out in the opening speeches. Such optimism proved to be partly misplaced.

To each of Cromwell's Protectorate parliaments there were returned a number of MPs—perhaps somewhere between 90 and 120 out of a possible 460—who held such pronounced and hostile politico-religious views that they were, or were believed to be, implacably opposed to the tenets of the Protectoral regime. It was these members, Sir Arthur Hesilrige, Thomas Scott and John Bradshaw to the fore, who launched a full-scale assault on the very foundations of the Instrument of Government during the opening week of the 1654 parliament. Many of them felt unable to sign the formal Recognition of the Protectoral government imposed by Cromwell nine days into the session and were thereafter excluded from the House. In 1656 members of this ilk were excluded from the very start, denied tickets of admission by the Council (Cromwell apparently had little to do with the process and was supposedly shocked and angry at the mass exclusions).[23] The admission of these MPs in January 1658 under the terms of the revised constitution largely explains why the mood of the second session was so different from that of the first and why the parliament ended after barely a fortnight of protest and disruption.

Up until the admission of the excluded members, the second Protectorate Parliament had been running quite smoothly. In the absence of so many constitutional opponents of the regime, the long first session was relatively orderly and productive. Much of the completed legislation answered or at least was consistent with the broad objectives sketched out in Cromwell's opening speech. A man could still be hanged for stealing sixpence, but other aspects of the legal system had been remodelled. MPs had done what they could to tighten security and to provide for the prosecution and vigorous punishment of the state's enemies. Acts against vagrants, for observation of the Lord's Day and so forth met Cromwell's call for moral reformation. Much of the incomplete legislation followed similar lines. MPs approved the Spanish war *nemine contradicente* after a brief debate in which hardly a word of criticism was apparently uttered. The House was not so quick or unstinting at providing financial assistance to pay for the war and other governmental needs, but by the beginning of 1657 MPs had begun to grant funds and the session ended with a flurry of adequate if not over-generous financial measures: acts continued tonnage and poundage, increased the excise, ordered a cash grant to be raised in Scotland, imposed a tax on buildings around London and not only extended the regular monthly assessments but also applied a second additional assessment specifically to cover the costs of the armed forces. Cromwell appeared unmoved at parliament's abolition of the system of the major-generals, and although he was undoubtedly angry and distressed at the prosecution and severe punishment of James Naylor—the over-enthusiastic Quaker who had ridden on a donkey into Bristol—Cromwell took no immediate action beyond addressing several curt letters to the Speaker. Moreover, he believed that provisions in the new constitution, chiefly the creation of a new second chamber, would render the repetition of such parliamentary persecution most unlikely. Some aspects of the Humble Petition, particularly kingship, caused uncertainty and heart-searching, but most of the new constitution matched Cromwell's own hopes and aspirations. By 1657 he was convinced that the Instrument of Government was deficient and in need of extensive revision and he welcomed the final versions of the Humble and Additional Petitions unreservedly. At last, his government would rest on a foundation endorsed by the people as represented in parliament. In June 1657 MPs were justifiably proud of their achievement and Cromwell, too, was full of praise.[24] He had let the session run for over nine months, well beyond the minimum duration for a parliament and far longer than contemporaries had predicted the previous autumn. The drastic reversals of fortunes in January 1658 and the sudden collapse of the second session can be attributed to personnel and policies almost entirely absent from the long first session. It is to the events of the second session that Cromwell pointed during his uncharacteristically brief speech of dissolution.[25]

For all the worthy legislation which it drafted, the first Protectorate Parliament had not been such a happy occasion. The session almost broke down within the first week, and although the imposition of the Recognition and the departure of the leading opponents of the regime went part way to healing the breach, disorder continued. MPs tried to meet most of Cromwell's vaguely annunciated requests: bills were introduced to reform parts of the legal system and to settle Ireland, diplomacy was encouraged, the preparation of the Western Expedition was respectfully left to Protector and Council, and Cromwell's appointees to senior offices of state were approved without a murmur.

Nor was constitutional reform anathema to the Protector. By autumn 1654 Cromwell may already have been aware of the defects inherent in the Instrument of Government. In his opening speech he implied that MPs should examine it and nine days later he explicitly allowed and invited its partial revision. Thereafter his agents in the House made no attempt to rush through acceptance of the Instrument *in toto* and Cromwell seems to have been quite willing for parliament to revise it, provided certain fundamental tenets were retained. Much of the resulting Government Bill was quite unexceptional, a schedule of sane and sensible provisions very similar to those of the Instrument and Humble Petition, both of which Cromwell accepted (in their final forms) without hesitation. There were heated exchanges in the chamber over the power to make peace and war, the hereditary or elective nature of the Protectorship, and the vaguely worded religious clauses, which gave rise to fears for future restrictions and persecutions; kingship briefly raised its disruptive head at the end of the year. Ultimately, however, it was none of these issues which divided Protector and parliament. It was the attempt of MPs, via the Government Bill and other draft legislation, drastically to reduce the size of the armed forces by slashing the military budget and to remove the guaranteed, permanent joint control of the Lord Protector over the regular forces and the militias, which led to a curt dissolution at the earliest opportunity, Cromwell angrily dismissing both parliament and its draft legislation as 'a threat to public interest and safety'.[26]

All of which begs the question, how was it that a purged parliament in 1656–7 worked in reasonable harmony with the Protector and the executive, producing a satisfactory draft constitution with adequate and acceptable provision for the command and pay of the existing forces, where a purged parliament in 1654–5 found the task impossible? Despite Trevor-Roper's claim to detect an organised party in the House during 1657, led by Lord Broghill and his associates, there is in reality little surviving evidence to suggest that the second Protectorate Parliament was generally better managed than the first. As we shall see, Cromwell's attempts at parliamentary management were very limited and produced meagre results. Rather, the difference probably lies in the weak opposition encountered in 1656–7. Kingship provoked bitter divisions in the House—'a pitch battle' one MP called it[27]—but most constitutional provisions, including those settling the military budget and confirming joint control, passed with the minimum of debate or dissent and often without formal division. Legislation detailing the sources and duration of the money grants was passed towards the end of the session, again with very limited dissent. Why was the opposition, so vocal and ultimately successful in 1654–5, so muted in 1656–7? In part, the answer lies in the changed circumstances. In the twenty months between his two Protectorate parliaments, Cromwell had made strenuous efforts to reduce the size and costs of the standing forces, within the limits of his own and the state's security requirements. In 1656 the size of the army was nearly 10,000 men down on the 1654 figure, and the annual bill was correspondingly lower. Moreover, a series of conspiracies and risings during 1655, most notably Penruddock's rebellion in the West Country, and the outbreak of formal war with Spain, brought home to MPs the need for large and adequately funded forces. But personnel as well as policies had changed by 1656–7.

We know quite a lot about the active membership of the 1656, and from a number of sources we can confidently identify just over 100 MPs excluded by the Council before the session opened. It is also well recorded that a further forty or more absented themselves in protest at the mass exclusion of their colleagues during the opening week, and rarely if ever returned during the remainder of the session.[28] Thus around 150 MPs, comprising those who were, or who were perceived to be, the most prominent opponents of the regime, were missing from the House throughout the session of 1656–7. Evidence for the 1654 parliament is not so plentiful—no contemporary list survives of those who took or refused the Recognition and Goddard's parliamentary diary only very rarely names individuals. In consequence, we are forced to rely heavily upon the uncertain evidence of nomination to committees and service as tellers in formal divisions, plus a variety of passing comments in newsletters. It is clear that no more than a handful of MPs were excluded from the House at the opening of the session and that most republicans and other political opponents and critics of the Protectorate were in their seats during the opening days of the session.[29] Identifying those subsequently excluded for failing to sign the 12 September Recognition is more difficult, though we can identify around 310 MPs who were apparently active in the House after that date—that is, they served as a teller or were nominated to a committee[30]—and a generally well informed diplomat claimed that by the end of October around 350 members had signed the Recognition.[31] Not all 460 seats were filled in 1654–5; some Scottish seats remained vacant and some of the double or treble returns appear never to have been resolved and to have produced the required by-elections. In addition, some of the absenteeism probably resulted from old age and ill health—at least three members died during the parliament[32]—rather than politically motivated opposition to the regime and its Recognition. Even allowing for this 'non-political' short-fall, Thurloe's boast that no more than thirty MPs had refused the Recognition is probably an exaggeration,[33] but the best guess would be that by November 1654 somewhere between fifty and eighty MPs were excluded from the House through politically motivated refusal to take the Recognition.

If the calculation that no more than eighty political opponents of the regime were absent from the 1654 parliament is correct, then this constitutes barely half the number who were excluded or who excluded themselves from the 1656–7 session. By itself, this goes a long way towards explaining the differences between the two sessions. In 1654 many critics of the Protectorate felt able to sign the Recognition, retook their seats and proceeded to mount vehement opposition to some elements of the constitution, most notably finance and military control. Having revealed their true colours in the first Protectorate Parliament, most of these critics (John and Thomas Birch, for example, Sir Ralph Hare, Herbert Morley, John Hobart and, from December 1654, Sir Anthony Ashley Cooper) as well as the diehard republicans who had withdrawn in September (Hesilrige, Scott, Bradshaw, John Weaver and the like) were excluded from the beginning in 1656. In total over sixty former members of the first Protectorate Parliament were elected to but barred from the second. Little wonder that opposition to the constitution was rather muted in 1656–7.

Exclusion leads on to the third and final aspect of these parliaments discussed here, namely control. In many ways, the barring of MPs from the House either at or just after the opening of the session was not only the most emphatic but also the most successful managerial tactic attempted throughout the period. It had a clear impact upon the ensuing sessions and made both Protectorate parliaments, but particularly the second, far more orderly than they would otherwise have been. Beyond that, surviving sources suggest that little was attempted and even less achieved. There is no sign of consistent or coherent parliamentary management, no evidence of carefully laid plans designed to guide the session along a predetermined path. At times, particularly during the 1654 parliament, one can identify the Protectoral or executive interests,

interests duly advanced, more often defended, by a group of agents and supporters in the House, a loose amalgam of councillor MPs, civilian office holders and army officers. In contemporary parlance, they were the 'courtiers' or 'court party' and their activities were noted by Goddard and, occasionally, by Burton in their parliamentary diaries. But this was far from a unified, long-term party. Rather, it was a temporary meeting of fellow travellers whose interests happened to coincide with each other's and with the Protector's. On many occasions and over many issues, there existed no courtier grouping and no clear Protectoral intentions. For example, the Protector's opinion of the hereditary or elective nature of his office, the offer of the crown and the system of local government headed by the major-generals was not apparent to contemporaries and remains uncertain. It was at the time and still remains now impossible to judge which side in the kingship controversy was furthering Cromwell's wishes and which thwarting them.

If Cromwell had no permanent party within the House, nor did any other individual or interest group. Opposition was frequently apparent and vociferous, but it was manifested as an *ad hoc* resistance to particular issues, not as an opposition, still less as the opposition. Meagre as it is, the evidence gleaned from the names of tellers and from a handful of division lists makes clear that the Protectoral parliaments were very fluid assemblies, composed of temporary and usually shortlived alliances briefly surfacing amid the ebb and flow of shifting interests and issues. Ashley Cooper's evolution from loyal Protectoral councillor to outspoken critic of the constitution during 1654 to excludee in 1656 was merely the most dramatic and conspicuous example of changing allegiances. Critics of the government in the first Protectorate Parliament show up as apparently loyal Protectoral men in the second; a few who apparently did not take the Recognition in 1654 were admitted in 1656 and seem to have played inconspicuous, innocuous roles; MPs who had obscure and apparently blameless records in 1654 were barred from the House two years later; members who worked together in one division counted for opposing sides in the next. In these circumstances, the terms 'court' and 'courtier' must be used with great caution, and 'country', 'Independent' and 'Presbyterian' are better avoided altogether. Nor are 'soldier' and 'civilian' particularly useful labels. It is notoriously difficult to be certain exactly who merited the designation soldier in the decade after the civil wars. Moreover, the vote on kingship in spring 1657 —almost the only division of the Protectorate for which we possess apparently full division lists[34] and the one usually described as revealing most clearly a military versus civilian split—in fact shows that, by any definition, the two 'parties' were nothing of the kind. Soldiers and civilians appear in strength on both sides.

Cromwell seems to have believed quite genuinely that his parliaments, purged perhaps but then left to their own devices, would work diligently and meet the needs of state and government for which they had been summoned. Further mortal interference and executive control would be inappropriate and unnecessary. In practice, Cromwell's principal potential agents in the House, the councillor MPs, seem to have attempted to exert control only during odd moments of crisis, by which time it was often too late to achieve anything. The results of this lack of central direction were mixed. In 1654–5 parliament produced policies ultimately unacceptable to the Protector, in 1656–7 a constitution and legislation generally satisfactory. And in any case, for much of the time, both parliaments were handling business which produced few serious divisions and which did little to disturb the relative harmony of the purged House. The discussion of petitions and deliberation of public and private legislation often provoked sharp words and heated exchanges, but rarely gave rise to a major, long-lasting conflict of interests or to a bitter power struggle for control of the House. In a chamber of fleeting divisions and perpetually shifting issues which broke the relative calm only intermittently and usually briefly, attempts at long-term parliamentary management and counter-management were naturally absent.

In addition, sheer inexperience probably contributed to the paucity of parliamentary management as well as to some of the inefficiencies of the Protectorate parliaments. A year older than the century, Cromwell was well versed in military command and army politics, but his experience even of local peacetime administration was limited and his parliamentary experience, though greater, was unbalanced. He had first entered the Commons in the 1628–9 parliament, when the relationship between crown and parliament was already in serious difficulties. After brief service in the Short Parliament, he was a member of the Long Parliament for over thirteen years, taking his seat whenever military duties permitted. Thus all his parliamentary experience had been pervaded by an atmosphere of crisis, war or constitutional novelty. Any picture he possessed of stable relations between parliament and head of state and of smooth management of a session by the executive was probably drawn from a semi-mythologised view of Elizabethan harmony and good government taken from a distant past beyond his own experience. This limited and slanted experience was shared by most of the Protectoral MPs. An analysis of the membership of the first Protectorate parliament reveals that, understandably perhaps, no Elizabethan MP had survived to sit in 1654–5, but nor had any member of James I's long first parliament; the link with Cecil and the supposed Jacobean swansong of Elizabethan management was lost. Indeed, the inexperience of the 1654–5 parliament is quite striking. Fewer than thirty MPs seem to have sat prior to 1640 and almost two-thirds of the members had no prior parliamentary experience of any kind. Most of the rest had first sat in the Long Parliament and, like Cromwell, were well versed in the politics of war and crisis, of a parliament in perpetual session and exercising both executive and legislative functions itself. Protector and parliament would be entering unfamiliar territory and would have to map out their roles, relationship and any management techniques anew.[35]

Trevor-Roper's image of these parliaments is of successive waves of politicians scrambling for the front benches in order to manage and control the session. In 1654, after the Recognition had removed the republicans, the old country party supposedly came to the fore under the leadership of John Birch, John Bulkeley and Sir Richard Onslow, who gained control of the House in the face of feeble courtier opposition led by Sir Charles Wolseley and, until his defection, Sir Anthony Ashley Cooper. In 1656–7 the country party and the new court allegedly came together to form a kingship party, led by Lord Broghill and supported by many of his fellow Irish MPs, which by a 'parliamentary coup' quickly took control of the House. Cromwell's eventual refusal of the crown brought the edifice crashing down and thus opened the way for the republican hijacking of the House during the brief second session. Much of the Trevor-Roper thesis is certainly true—the very limited nature of Cromwell's parliamentary management, the republican domination of the opening days of the first Protectorate Parliament and the second session of the second, the generally critical attitude of the 1654–5 parliament even after the removal of certain opponents via the Recognition. But the thesis also contains sweeping over-simplifications. Both parliaments seem to have been fluid assemblies, with shifting allegiances amidst a diversity of issues. Trevor-Roper's portrayal of the 1656–7 session as dominated by Broghill's 'kingship party' seems particularly sweeping. During a nine-month session, the kingship issue was in fact debated on less than ten days between the presentation of the

Remonstrance in late February and Cromwell's final refusal of the crown, in early May. While there is no doubt that Broghill actively favoured the offer of the crown, Burton's parliamentary diary does not suggest that he led the House, either during the kingship debates or at other times during the session. According to the Commons Journals, Broghill served as a teller just four times throughout the session, far less often than a host of well known and not so well known MPs, and an examination of the number of times he was nominated to committees compared to the records of other members reveals that he came a glorious thirty-sixth in a league table of nominations, again appearing far less often than many seemingly less distinguished MPs. The frequency of such nominations, quite high during the opening months of the parliament, fell away sharply during spring 1657, the very time that kingship came to the fore, and thereafter remained quite low. The evidence of the Commons Journals indicates that Broghill was more active and prominent in the first Protectorate Parliament than the second.

Yet Trevor-Roper is undoubtedly correct in suggesting that, whether through ignorance and inexperience, an undue optimism that MPs would share his goals and aspirations, or a deeply held belief that he should not attempt to influence the workings of a 'free' parliament, Cromwell and his agents attempted only fitfully and often unsuccessfully to guide and manage his Protectoral parliaments. Potentially, his principal agents in the House were the members of his Council. The two aristocratic councillors, Edmund Sheffield, second Earl of Mulgrave, and Philip Sidney, Viscount Lisle and heir to the earldom of Leicester, declined to stand, though they were not constitutionally barred from the House and a handful of peers were elected to the two Protectoral parliaments. The remaining councillors all stood and were returned to parliament in 1654 and 1656, creating a potential block of parliamentary managers. In reality, they formed no such thing. Some of them were clearly absent from the House for long periods: old Richard Maijor soon tired of proceedings and shuffled off to his Hampshire estates, Edward Montagu went to Huntingdonshire to 'take air' after his exertions at sea, Charles Fleetwood was in Ireland throughout the first Protectorate Parliament, Francis Rous and Philip Skippon were often absent nursing frail health and old bodies. The parliamentary diaries, especially Burton's of 1656–7, indicate that some councillors spoke frequently, others rarely or never. Although, taken as a group, the councillor MPs come across in the Commons Journals as slightly more active than the norm, closer examination reveals huge discrepancies. The frequency with which councillors served as tellers or were nominated to committees varied enormously, some (Wolseley, Philip Jones and John Disbrowe, for example) appearing amongst the more energetic and prominent MPs in the House, others (such as Henry Lawrence) so inconspicuous as to be almost invisible.

Moreover, even when councillor MPs were active, they often opposed each other or the Protector. Given the nature of the surviving sources, we know far more about such matters in the second Protectorate Parliament than in the first. During the session of 1656–7, councillor MPs served as tellers in fifty divisions; in eleven of these, they opposed each other, counting on different sides. The councillor MPs were unusually prominent in the debates on Naylor during December 1656, but they were divided, albeit unequally, with Rous and Skippon rousing themselves in uncharacteristic activity to condemn Naylor, and the remainder, reflecting Cromwell's own views, urging moderation and caution. On the issue of the Militia Bill, which would have confirmed the sysyem of the major-generals and the decimation tax, the councillors were more united, most supporting the bill on the floor of the House or in divisions, the remainder staying silent; according to the available records, no councillor MP clearly opposed the Militia Bill when it was debated between late December 1656 and late January 1657. However, in this case it is not at all clear that the councillors were thereby reflecting the wishes of the head of state and were guiding the House along the Protector's preferred path. Cromwell's ostentatious support for one of the leading critics of the Militia Bill and his subsequent criticism of its introduction suggest that councillor MPs were trying to lead the House along paths neither approved nor desired by the Protector. The councillor MPs were again split during spring 1657, when the proposal to give Cromwell the crown came before the House, but this time far more seriously, with six opposing kingship and six supporting it.[36] The body of men who were most likely to act as Protectoral managers in the House were, in reality, split down the middle and vigorously confronting each other. Cromwell's own views of kingship remain obscure, but whatever his true feelings, at least half his councillor MPs must have been attempting to guide the House in a contrary direction.[37]

However, the story is more complex than this, for Cromwell did occasionally attempt to manage his Protectoral parliaments, and his agents in the House, principally the councillor MPs, did occasionally attempt, sometimes successfully, sometimes not, to lead their colleagues along a predetermined path. Moreover, for all Cromwell's inexperience and perhaps his genuine desire to hold back from influencing parliament, lessons were learnt from the shortcomings of the first Protectorate Parliament and there were clear if shortlived attempts to improve the management of the second Protectorate Parliament. Attempts at such parliamentary management were generally undertaken to avert an impending crisis or to defuse an actual crisis. Here it is instructive to compare the opening days of the two parliaments.

The first week or so of the first Protectorate Parliament was strewn with examples of mismanagement and misjudgement, which led to crisis and a partial breakdown of relations between Protector and parliament. The intention was that no work be done on the opening day, Sunday 3 September. Instead MPs would attend church and then hear a short speech from the Protector asking them to adjourn to the following day, when he would make his full opening speech and work would begin. But after returning from the Abbey, MPs were left sitting in the chamber for up to an hour before being summoned to hear Cromwell. This allowed the House to hold a rambling debate. The lawfulness of meeting on a Sunday, the authority by which they had been called together and the legitimacy of the Instrument were all discussed, and when MPs got round to pondering the choice of Speaker the candidates included John Bradshaw, a leading opponent of the regime. Fortunately for Cromwell, no decision had been reached when the message arrived summoning MPs to hear his short speech; equally fortunately, members broke off their debate and attended Cromwell in the Painted Chamber, despite cries of 'sit still' from a dozen or so of their colleagues. It was not an auspicious beginning.

Over the subsequent week, MPs began examining the Instrument of Government in detail. Cromwell probably wanted speedy and almost unquestioning acceptance and confirmation of the existing constitution from his parliament, but this proved a misguided and unrealistic aspiration. His agents in the House, 'divers eminent persons of State' as one contemporary report has it, opened the debates on 5 and 6 September, the first full working days of the session, by urging speedy approval of 'the Protector's power'. But they met strong and equally vocal opposition, the leading critics of the regime skilfully deploying a range of delaying tactics—proposing that religion be discussed first, sidetracking the issue by having a whole day spent in a debate over whether the Treason Ordinance hindered free speech in parliament, and on 7 September successfully moving that the Instrument be considered in Grand Committee, where the formal rules of debate were relaxed and a member could speak as often as he wished, a recipe for long and largely uncontrolled discussion. Although the 'courtiers' tried to defend the constitution, the mood in Grand Committee swung heavily against the regime on 8 and 9 September, with sweeping attacks made upon elements of the Instrument and proposals for a new constitution to be drawn up in which the Protector—if such an office survived—would lose many of his powers. The 'courtiers' did attempt to reach a compromise settlement on Monday 11 September, proposing that if the House accept certain 'fundamental' elements—government by Protector and non-perpetual parliaments, joint control over armed forces and over religion—all other constitutional issues could be discussed. But the compromise plan offered too little too late, it was brushed aside by the critics of the regime and instead Cromwell was forced to intervene directly, temporarily closing the House on 12 September and imposing the Recognition.

That the 'courtiers' had been able on 11 September to present what appear from the surviving parliamentary diary to have been long, lucid and well-prepared arguments, knowing what to concede and what to retain as the minimum acceptable, suggests careful and quite detailed advanced planning. That they could confidently concede so much but pick upon the very same 'fundamentals' which Cromwell would lay down in his speech on the 12th, suggests that the Protector had discussed the position with his councillor MPs and other leading supporters in advance, probably over the weekend of 9–10 September. But by then it was too late to retrieve the situation without external intervention and tests. The impression given by the surviving sources is that the Protector and his agents in the House, principally his councillor MPs, had been unprepared and caught off-guard by the vehemence and tactics employed by opponents of the regime and had completely lost control of the session during the opening week.[38]

The first week or so of the second Protectorate Parliament presents a very different picture. On this occasion, councillor MPs and others knew that they would have to contain a potentially very divisive issue, namely the pre-session exclusion of around 100 MPs, and quickly move the admitted MPs to embark upon normal parliamentary business. Sure enough, on 18 September, the first working day of the session, a letter of complaint from some of the excluded members was presented, heralding a four-day debate on exclusions. The councillor MPs confirmed that they had excluded the MPs under the terms of the written constitution, Nathaniel Fiennes taking the lead in explaining the Council's actions in line with a written statement prepared by the Council at an early morning meeting on 22 September. Despite some fierce attacks on the Council's actions during that day's debates, the councillor MPs and other Protectoral agents acted to bring the issue to a swift conclusion, determined to prevent opponents spinning out debates or placing the matter in Grand Committee. Two councillor MPs, Fiennes and Disbrowe, counted as tellers and in the division had a comfortable 35-vote majority over opposition moves to adjourn. John Lambert and Lord Broghill then counted a majority of nearly 100 in favour of a resolution that the excluded members should apply to Council and that the House should proceed with business. Although some other MPs withdrew before and after this division in protest at the exclusions, the danger was over and, with several councillor MPs prominent in debate, the House had been persuaded to acquiesce in the exclusions.

At the same time, the councillor MPs were active in moving the House onto other business, principally the discussion of legislation desired by and helpful to the regime. On 18 September Wolseley had presented a bill for 'removing and disannulling the pretended title of Charles Stuart'—a clever move, for even those MPs who had reservations about the existing regime could hardly oppose the bill, even though it would implicitly recognise the Protector and his government. Although there is no firm evidence to show who introduced the bill for 'the security of the Lord Protector' on 23 September, it seems probably that this was also an 'official' measure; again, although the ostensible aim of the legislation was the strengthening of state security, it would also bring with it further parliamentary acceptance of the existing regime. The government legislative programme seems to have gone no further than this, and further bills introduced during the succeeding weeks appear to have been initiated by individual MPs or committees of MPs. Equally, the management of the councillor MPs and other protectoral agents in the House soon ran into the sand. We have already seen how the session was allowed to run on during the autumn in a worthy but apparently unstructured way and how in several of the subsequent issues, especially the Naylor case and kingship, Councillor MPs were divided and opposed each other. None the less, the way in which the explosive issue of exclusions had been contained and defused at the start of the session and the House quickly moved on to embark on legislation helpful to the regime is very different from the chaotic opening to the first Protectorate Parliament and shows that some lessons had been learnt.[39]

Oliver Cromwell's two Protectorate parliaments can be portrayed as failures. Both were purged and both ended in abrupt, angry dissolutions. The Government Bill, upon which the first lavished so much time and effort, was immediately discarded; of the fruit borne by the second Protectorate Parliament, its revised written constitution survived less than two years and its legislation was wiped from the statute book at the Restoration. But two important correctives need to be added to this bleak image. Firstly, there is a positive side to these parliaments, a picture of MPs attempting to fulfil the traditional and constructive role of an early modern parliament in new and difficult circumstances, to meet the needs of the state and at least some of the aspirations of the head of state, and to strengthen and secure the nation against enemies at home and abroad. Some of the attempts were unsuccessful or half-hearted, but business was conducted, legislation was prepared and the ship of state was kept afloat. Oliver Cromwell's Protectorate came to end, not through any act of parliamentary omission or commission, but by natural causes. Secondly, such failures as did occur were brought about by far more than Cromwell's inability to understand and employ the management techniques supposedly used by his Tudor and Stuart predecessors. Occasionally Cromwell was able and willing to manage the parliament, in his own way, and to use his councillor MPs and others to guide the House. Instead, the shortcoming of these parliaments can be ascribed to the complex legacy of the civil wars, to the inexperience of all concerned —MPs as well as Protector—for anything other than the politics of division and novelty which had pervaded parliamentary politics since 1640, if not before, and to Cromwell's genuine and deeply held belief that he should not attempt to influence the workings of a 'free' parliament, a belief perhaps born of an undue optimism that MPs would share his goals and aspirations and that God's will would prevail. The story of Cromwell and his Protectorate parliaments is not so much a tragi-comedy or a simple tale of mismanagement in the traditional sense; rather, it is a complex story of partial successes leavened by the failures inherent in the divergent experiences, ideas and aspirations of men. Accordingly, and despite all the constitutional novelties of the 1650s, the two Protectorate parliaments have much in common with a typical early modern English parliament.

Notes

1. H. R. Trevor-Roper, 'Oliver Cromwell and his Parliament', originally appeared in R. Pares and A. J. P. Taylor (eds), *Essays Presented to Sir Lewis Namier* (London, 1956). It appeared in a slightly revised form in H. R. Trevor-Roper, *Religion, the Reformation and Social Change* (London, 1967).
2. See the pamphlets and other material in the Thomason Collection at the British Library. Modern assessments of contemporary and near contemporary views of Cromwell include John Morrill, 'Cromwell and his Contemporaries' in John Morrill (ed.), *Oliver Cromwell and the English Revolution* (London, 1990) and Roger Howell, ' "That imp of Satan": the Restoration image of Cromwell' in R. C. Richardson (ed.), *Images of Oliver Cromwell* (Manchester, 1993).
3. For Cromwell's political views in context, see Johann Sommerville, 'Oliver Cromwell and English Political Thought' in Morrill (ed.), *Oliver Cromwell and the English Revolution*.
4. Austin Woolrych poses the question 'The Cromwellian Protectorate: A Military Dictatorship?' and answers it firmly in the negative in *History*, 75 (1990).
5. The most accessible text of this speech is in Ivan Roots (ed.), *Speeches of Oliver Cromwell* (London, 1989), pp. 28–40.
6. See Peter Gaunt, 'The Councils of the Protectorate, from December 1653 to September 1658' (unpublished PhD thesis, University of Exeter, 1983), chapter 7; Gaunt, ' "The Single Person's Confidants and Dependants"?: Oliver Cromwell and his Protectoral Councillors', *Historical Journal*, 32 (1989), and Roots (ed.), *Speeches of Oliver Cromwell*, pp. 79–106.
7. See Gaunt, 'The Councils of the Protectorate', chapter 8, and Gaunt, ' "The Single Person's Confidants and Dependants"?'
8. David Underdown, *Pride's Purge* (Oxford, 1971). See also J. S. A. Adamson, 'Oliver Cromwell and the Long Parliament' in Morrill (ed.), *Oliver Cromwell and the English Revolution*.
9. A. B. Worden, *The Rump Parliament* (Cambridge, 1974).
10. Austin Woolrych, *Commonwealth to Protectorate* (Oxford, 1982).
11. S. R. Gardiner, *The History of the Commonwealth and Protectorate*, 4 vols (London, 1903); Vol. iii covers the first Protectorate Parliament and Vol iv looks at the elections to the second, but ends before the parliament opens. The two sessions of the second Protectorate Parliament are assessed by C. H. Firth, *The Last Years of the Protectorate*, 2 vols (London, 1909).
12. Peter Gaunt, 'Cromwell's Purge? Exclusions and the First Protectorate Parliament', *Parliamentary History*, 6 (1987); Gaunt, 'Law-Making in the First Protectorate Parliament'; Ivan Roots, 'Lawmaking in the Second

Protectorate Parliament' in H. Hearder and H. R. Loyn (eds), *British Government and Administration* (Cardiff, 1974); T. A. Wilson and F. J. Merli, 'Naylor's Case and the Dilemma of the Protectorate', *University of Birmingham Historical Journal*, 10 (1965–6); C. H. Firth, 'Cromwell and the Crown', *English Historical Review*, 17 (1902) and 18 (1903).

13. S. E. Jones, 'The Composition and Activity of the Protectorate Parliaments' (unpublished PhD thesis, University of Exeter, 1988).

14. Roger Howell, 'Cromwell and his Parliaments: the Trevor-Roper Thesis Revisited', *Cromwelliana* (1987–88), reprinted in Richardson (ed.), *Images of Oliver Cromwell*.

15. The two constitutions are printed in full in S. R. Gardiner, *Constitutional Documents of the Puritan Revolution* (Oxford, 1906).

16. Roots, 'Lawmaking in the Second Protectorate Parliament'. The main primary sources for this parliament are J. T. Rutt (ed.), *The Diary of Thomas Burton, Esq*, 4 vols (London, 1828), Vols i and ii, and *Commons Journal* vii, pp. 423–592. All subsequent comments about activities of MPs in making speeches, serving as tellers and being nominated to committees in this parliament are drawn from these two sources.

17. Thomas Carlyle, *Oliver Cromwell's Letters and Speeches*, revised edn in 3 vols (London, 1907), Vol. iii, p. 86.

18. The main primary sources for the first Protectorate Parliament are Goddard's diary printed in Rutt (ed.), *Diary of Thomas Burton*, Vol. i, and *Commons Journal* vii, pp. 365–421. All subsequent comments about the activities of MPs in making speeches, serving as tellers and being nominated to committees in this parliament are drawn from these two sources.

19. Cromwell's speeches to parliament are all printed in Roots (ed.), *Speeches of Oliver Cromwell*. All the quoted passages are taken from these speeches.

20. Ibid.

21. Ibid, pp. 28–40, 79–106.

22. Thomas Birch (ed.), *A Collection of the State Papers of John Thurloe, Esq*, 7 vols (London, 1742), Vol. v, p. 692.

23. See Gaunt, ' "The Single Person's Confidants and Dependants"?' for a detailed discussion of this point.

24. See his speeches in Roots (ed.), *Speeches of Oliver Cromwell*, pp. 166–8.

25. For the second session, see ibid, pp. 173–93.

26. Ibid, pp. 57–77.

27. British Library, Lansdowne Ms 822, ff. 3–4.

28. See Gaunt, 'The Councils of the Protectorate', chapter 7 and appendix C for a detailed discussion of the sources and their interpretation.

29. Gaunt, 'Cromwell's Purge?'

30. *Commons Journal* vii, pp. 367–421.

31. Nieuport's dispatch of 27 October/6 November at British Library, Additional

Ms 17677 U, f. 437, cited by Gardiner, *History of the Commonwealth and Protectorate*, Vol. iii, p. 203 n. 3.

32. Humphrey Mackworth, Sir Thomas Pelham and Henry Shelley. Nathaniel Barton was found to have taken holy orders and so was disqualified from sitting.

33. Thurloe to Pell, 24 October, in Richard Vaughan, *The Protectorate of Oliver Cromwell and the State of Europe during the Early Part of the Reign of Louis XIV*, 2 vols (London, 1838), Vol. i, p. 71.

34. T. Park (ed.), *Harleian Miscellany or a Collection of Scarce, Curious and Entertaining Pamphlets and Tracts*, 12 vols (London, 1807–11), Vol. vi, pp. 473—5. *The Parliamentary or Constitutional History of England*, 24 vols (London, 1751–63), Vol. xxi, pp. 3–23.

35. This information is drawn from my own trawl through the various secondary works on the parliaments and their membership c. 1580–1653. When published, the History of Parliament volumes covering the Protectorate parliaments will doubtless provide precise figures for previous parliamentary experience and will correct my rather rough calculations.

36. Confirmed not only by the division lists (see n. 34 above) but also by correspondence at British Library, Lansdowne Ms 821, ff. 294–5.

37. This account of the councillor MPs and their activities in the Protectorate parliaments is drawn from Gaunt, 'The Councils of the Protectorate', chapters 5 and 7 and the sources there cited.

38. This account of the events of 3–12 September is taken from Gaunt, 'The Councils of the Protectorate', pp. 132–5 and the sources there cited, principally *Commons Journal* vii, pp. 365–7, and Rutt (ed.), *Diary of Thomas Burton*, Vol. i, pp. xvii–xxxv.

39. This account of the events of the opening week of the second Protectorate parliament is taken from Gaunt, 'The Councils of the Protectorate', pp. 189–90 and 194 and the sources there cited, especially *Commons Journal* vii, pp. 423–6, and from Gaunt, ' "The Single Person's Confidants and Dependants"?', pp. 555–6.

5

The Politics of the Army and the Quest for Settlement

Derek Massarella

Introduction

The politics of the 1650s are no longer seen by historians merely as an epilogue to the civil war and prologue to the Restoration of the Stuarts in 1660. Settlement is seen as having been feasible, and for a short time under the Protectorate a substantial number of the traditional political nation appeared to be playing a more constructive role in politics.[1] In any discussion of the attempts made to secure a settlement of the division that resulted from the civil wars and the revolution of 1648–9, an understanding of the role of the army is crucial. The army, an institution unprecedented in English history, made the revolution of 1648–49, but it also made the Restoration of 1660, and its presence was impressed upon all the developments of the intervening years.

The creation of the New Model Army

The New Model Army was established by parliamentary Ordinance in January 1645. The traditional explanation of its creation was that it was part of an attempt to improve parliament's fighting ability by establishing

I would like to thank Professor G. E. Aylmer, Professor I. Roots and Dr Anne Lawrence for their comments on an earlier draft. The final version is, of course, my responsibility.

a national army with a unified structure directly under parliament's control, to replace the existing mixture of armies, which had regional rather than national loyalties, and which were headed by commanders who were reluctant to act in concert.[2] This assessment has been revised. Professor Mark Kishlansky suggests that the New Model did not mark a decisive break in the conduct of the parliamentary war effort, that its membership, structure and financing differed little from previous armies, and that despite a lower level of desertion than its royalist foes, the New Model's cohesion and performance owed more to luck—the need to engage the King at Naseby—than to any ideological, including religious, commitment on the part of its members. For Kishlansky, the creation of the New Model was the last act in the 'consensus decision making' process he suggests characterises the parliamentary war effort until 1645.[3] Such a revision has been challenged by Professors Austin Woolrych and Ian Gentles. Gentles argues that the Lords and Commons were divided along political and religious lines over the formation of the New Model.[4] Whether or not we subscribe to the view that the creation of the New Model marked a decisive turning point in the conduct of the war, we do know that many of its members, especially among the officer corps, were volunteers who felt that they *were* fighting for a cause. Indeed, one of the most obvious things about the civil war is that besides being a struggle for power brought about by the collapse of the King's government, it was also fought over issues of principle. Those who took up arms voluntarily did so to see those issues settled, no matter that the heat and dust of battle obscured differences of opinion among them about the nature of the eventual settlement.[5] Such active engagement to a cause is central to an understanding of why the army became a political force in 1647 and why it remained one throughout the 1650s.

The politicisation of the army

The army emerged as a political force during the spring and early summer of 1647 after victory in the field had been won. By March 1647 parliament, which was dominated by the Presbyterian peace party under the leadership of Denzil Holles and Sir Philip Stapleton, was intent on sending a part of the army to Ireland to quell the rebellion which had broken out there in 1641, maintaining some units in England and disbanding the rest. Holles, Stapleton and their supporters felt that such action would remove what they considered to be one of the greatest impediments in the way to reaching an accord with the King.[6] What they did not reckon on was the reaction within the army against these proposals.

At first the army opposed the terms for the Irish service on the grounds that they made inadequate provision for arrears, that they lacked indemnity for acts committed during the war and that they did not deal with other professional grievances. The initial impetus for this opposition came from the rank and file, but many of the officers shared the fears of the men. A sizeable number of the officers, however, were prepared to accept parliament's terms. These became known as 'undertakers'. Under the influence of external propaganda, most of which emanated from the London Levellers, who were quick to sense an opportunity, and fired by its own indignation, the majority of the army dug in its heels and refused to comply with the parliament's orders. By June with the King under army jurisdiction—he had been seized by a troop of horse under Cornet George Joyce in an action which was not ordered by the senior command, or grandees, but which had afterwards been condoned and exploited by them—and with the undertaker officers having decided to leave, the army claimed that it was not defying parliament merely to further its own ends, but that it was standing up for the interests of the nation as well. The claim was made succinctly on 14 June in *A Declaration or representation from His Excellency Sir Thomas Fairfax, and of the army under his command.* The army asserted 'that we are not a mere mercenary army, hired to serve any arbitrary power of a state, but called forth and conjured by the several Declarations of Parliament to the defence of our own and people's just rights and liberties'.[7] What had started out as essentially material grievances had 'become political ones; the army had entered national politics as a political force.

It soon became confident enough to draw up its own programme for settlement—the Heads of the Proposals, the work of Commissary General Henry Ireton and Colonel John Lambert, two of the most politically gifted members of the army[8]—and to negotiate directly with the King. In late July and early August—by which time Fairfax had been made Commander-in-Chief of all land forces in England and Wales—the army became involved in the first of many struggles to shape the nation's political future.

On 6 August it marched into London to defeat a Presbyterian attempt to seize power which had resulted in over seventy MPs, including the

Speaker, either fleeing to the army or signing a declaration calling on the army to intervene. Its response set the character for future interventions. It showed that the army did not aim at seizing power to install itself and to impose a settlement on the nation in the manner of modern military dictatorships, although this was by no means clear to all contemporaries. It also showed that by wielding the sword the army could guarantee security and had acquired a unique political strength that would enable it to become the ultimate arbiter about what sort of government was established. The point was put by Major Francis White of Fairfax's foot regiment, who said before the General Council of the Army in September that the army was 'the highest power visible in this kingdom, and if you see not a good Government established for the weale of the people, according to equity and reason, it will lye upon your Excellencie's and the Armye's account'.[9] White's analysis, however much truth there was in it, was too unsubtle for many of his colleagues and he was expelled from the Army Council, although other criticisms of the grandees' policy he expressed also played a part in this. He was re-admitted to the Council in December.

The Levellers had directed a lot of propaganda at the army since the spring and, despite the fact that two of their leaders, John Lilburne and Richard Overton, were in the Tower, they remained politically important. Over the summer of 1647 the Levellers grew suspicious of the continued negotiations between the grandees and the King over the Heads of the Proposals. These negotiations were soon to break down anyway because of Charles I's intransigence and his belief that he could always give little and gain most by playing off one group against the other. The Levellers were also critical of the lack of progress in dealing with the leaders of the Presbyterian attempted coup. They feared that the grandees would sell out to the King. To avoid this, they judged that the army needed to be pushed further to the left in the hope that it could be used as a launching pad to implement their own programme for settlement, based on the Agreement of the People.

With Leveller encouragement, some of the regiments chose new agitators, or agents as they were termed, to replace the existing agitators ejected by each regiment who sat as members of the Army Council. This body, whose function it was to debate army policy and which consisted of general officers, agitators and elected officers from the regiments, had been envisaged in the Solemn Engagement of the Army, drawn up in early June.[10] The Levellers alleged that the agitators had become puppets of the grandees. Despite their success in having some of their proposals discussed at the famous debates at Putney in October, the Levellers decided to challenge the grandees. Leveller supporters in the army, with the prompting of the London Levellers, called for a general rendezvous of the army. They hoped to use the occasion to try to swing the army behind the Agreement of the People and down a path far different from that being marked out by the grandees. The army leadership refused to concede to a call for a general rendezvous, and instead decided that there should be three separate rendezvous which would obviously be easier to control. At the first rendezvous, at Ware on 15 November, seven regiments were designated to participate but they were joined, contrary to orders, by two more, some of whose members wore copies of the Agreement in their hats. The regiments were urged to stand up for the Agreement, but order and discipline were quickly restored with Cromwell playing a leading part. The other two rendezvous, on 17 and 18 November, passed without incident. The débâcle at Ware resolved the issue of control within the army. That was to remain decisively with the officers and not to come from below; nor were the officers to be dictated to from outside. The Levellers failed to drum up enough support within the army, and almost all of the officer corps, some of which had certainly sympathised with the Leveller aims, closed ranks and ruthlessly put down this threat to army unity. A small number of officers openly sided with the Levellers at the time of Ware, the most notable of whom was Colonel Thomas Rainborowe (or Rainsborough). But in the aftermath of the mutiny, the mood was one of reconciliation and the officers, at least, were treated leniently and remained in the army. Ware ensured that the need to preserve army unity remained one of the sacred principles of army policy over the next decade. The importance of unity was expressed in an address to Fairfax from the regiment of Colonel Robert Lilburne (elder brother of the Leveller John, although he did not share his younger brother's views), one of the mutinous regiments involved in the Ware episode. The regiment declared that 'as soldiers . . . we owe all Obedience and Subjection to your Excellency's Authorities and Commands; from which we humbly conceive neither Birthrights, nor other Priveledges whatsoever, whereof we have or ought to have an equal share with others, can or ought in the least to disoblige us'.[11]

The army emerges as a revolutionary force

Regardless of the Levellers' attempt to whip up the army, there had been a shift to the left anyway during the course of the year. This was in response to a variety of factors of which the Levellers were only one. The others were the Presbyterian-controlled parliament, the King, the City of London and developments with the army itself. The army felt obliged to respond to these threats even if this involved more than just a questioning of traditional authority but an actual challenge to it.

After Ware there was no easing up on the army's desire to see the achievement of a satisfactory political settlement. During the early winter there was a period of harmony between the parliament, in which the Presbyterians had suffered an eclipse of their power, and the army. This harmony survived into the new year, although by the outbreak of the second civil war serious difference had appeared over the question of settlement and the part of Charles I in that settlement. Since Ware the grandees, reflecting sentiment within the army, had hardened their attitude towards further dealings with the King. This was stiffened even more in December by the King's rejection of the Four Bills, covering parliamentary control of the militia for twenty years, the revocation of declarations against parliament, the annulment of recent royal grants and honours, and royal assent to parliament's right to adjourn to whatever place it felt fit. The Four Bills were designed as a *sine qua non* for further negotiations. Charles's confident rejection of the Bills, inspired by his decision to throw in his lot with the Scots in the desperate belief that they would re-establish him on the throne, led to the passing of the Vote of No Addresses in January 1648. The decision of the Commons on 28 April to suspend this vote led to the deterioration of relations between army and parliament. At a prayer meeting at Windsor in late April 1648—prayer meetings often preceded important decisions or changes in policy—the officers decided that Charles Stuart, 'that Man of Blood', should be brought to account 'for that Blood he had shed, and Mischief he had done to his utmost against the Lord's cause and People in these poor Nations'.[12]

It was a momentous decision and marks the army's emergence as a revolutionary force, not just a radical political one. But the decision meant that the army was in danger of manoeuvring itself into political isolation. The trial of the King was unlikely to find widespread support at Westminster, especially amongst the middle group, which had generally supported the army, let alone in the country. It also appeared that the constitutional settlement based on the Heads of the Proposals was being quietly abandoned, unless it was intended to substitute another member of the royal family as monarch, but there was no suggestion of this. The co-operation between parliament and army manifest in December and January had evaporated. In its place there was now an impasse that was only to be removed by the follies of the second civil war, which pushed the army even further to the left and into a committed revolutionary position from which it was instrumental in bringing about not just the King's trial but his execution and also in ushering in the new Republic.

The army and the revolution of 1648–1649

The need to fight a second civil war, during which time the Presbyterians were able to stage a comeback and to secure middle group support for fresh negotiations with the King (the Treaty of Newport), had ensured that the army did not cast away the revolutionary mantle it had donned in April. Rhetoric was transformed into action. Parliament was purged, the King brought to trial and executed, the Lords abolished and England declared a Commonwealth. At the end of August 1648 Elizabeth, Countess Dowager of Lindsay, had written to Lord Montagu declaring that 'The Army is now master of the kingdom'.[13] Her observation was perhaps inaccurate when it was written—the struggle over the Treaty of Newport still lay ahead—yet it seemed a fair enough description of the state of affairs in February 1649. Or was it?

The army had certainly brought about the revolution; but it had not done so alone. It had worked closely with civilians, both parliamentary and non-parliamentary, including the Levellers whose influence and ideas had continued to be felt in the army despite Ware. But although Levellers were an important factor in the calculations of the army leadership and their ideas were treated seriously at the time of the revolution in late 1648 and early 1649, they did not aim to outbid the officers for rank-and-file support at that time as they had tried to in 1647. Thus the army had not seized power unilaterally, carried out a revolution and proceeded to attempt to force a settlement on the nation. During the revolution no army dictator emerged and no individual officer masterminded the army's policy. Cromwell stayed clear of London until after Pride's Purge; Ireton, one of the most important officers shaping policy, did not display any personal ambitions during the revolutionary months; Fairfax, an excellent military commander but a weak politician, preferred to remain in the background. In fact the army leadership did everything possible to ensure that the revolution would be limited and that hopefully it would not alienate too many among the political nation. It sought to legitimise the revolution and to further it by making these tasks the responsibility primarily of civilians and not solely of army officers. The army's own proposals for settlement, which were debated by a General Council of Officers in December 1648 and January 1649 (soldiers had not been admitted to debates since January 1648) and eventually spelt out in the so-called 'officers' Agreement', were presented to parliament for that body to consider and to implement.[14] The army did not want its actions and role to be interpreted as an attempt to set itself up in power.

But there had been a debate within the officer corps about how far the revolution should proceed and about how far the army should be prepared to advance it. It was a debate largely over means not ends and was thus very different from the one which had caused the split between undertaker and non- undertaker officers in 1647. During the discussions, which were held at Whitehall, Captain George Joyce—the man who had seized the King in 1647 and since been promoted—declared that he did not doubt 'that if there was nott a spiritt of feare upon your Excellency [Fairfax] and the Councill [of Officers], that he [the Lord] would make you instruments to the people of these thinges that hee hath sett before you'. His argument was countered by Colonel Thomas Harrison in a long speech, which partly paraphrases the Declaration preceding the officers' Agreement, in which he asserted that even if, as was inevitable, the Agreement fell short of satisfying all of the godly, especially in religious questions, it would be a proof that the army did not intend to seize power for itself:

> For itt is nott a principle of man, when wee have brought downe such men that would have kept us under, to give them a libertie, butt itt is more of God, to putt them into such a condition especially as to thinges of civill concernment that wee neede not seeks ourselves, that wee will trust God and give them uppe in a common current againe.[15]

For Harrison this was a fundamentally different position from that which he came to hold by 1653. In 1649, like Cromwell and Ireton, he was expressing the assumption that guided army policy at this time. All three supported and advocated a more limited revolution, not a more thoroughgoing one which might have sought to establish new institutions designed to reflect or even rubber-stamp the army's demands. The latter course is one which most modern military interventions in politics have attempted to follow in different fashions regardless of whether or not an obvious military dictator has emerged. The English Revolution was different.

In its propaganda, the army had emphasised that it had fought to defend the people's rights and liberties. These were not empty words. The experience of battle and latterly of political engagement had given its members a sense of identity and purpose. But unlike modern armies, the New Model did not live apart from the people, closeted in barracks. It lived among them, dependent on them for food and lodging. The army did not consider itself as a separate estate. Had it done so, it would have been easier to dictate a settlement and use the sword to enforce it. But such a course of action was impossible for the army leadership to contemplate. The New Model was a first generation army, its commanders volunteers. An ambiguity was etched across its heart making it impossible to categorise its leaders neatly as either military or civilian in outlook or behaviour: Fairfax, uncomfortable centre stage in a political drama that tore at his troubled conscience, relief coming only through resignation from his command and withdrawal from political life; Ireton, haranguing the Levellers at Putney in words and manner more befitting a landed gentleman than a career army officer; Harrison, the glint of the Millenium in his eye, preferring the company of the Saints before his military career and thereby steering himself into political oblivion; and the supreme case of ambiguity, Cromwell himself, military commander and civilian politician, drawing his political strength from both capacities but never independent of either and hence weakened by the conflicting loyalties that they aroused. During the 1650s the self-perception persisted within the army that it was indivisible from the people, but for most civilians this was seen otherwise, as self-deception by an institution that despite its rhetoric had become *de facto* a separate estate.

The army and the Rump

The need to secure the revolution against enemies at home and abroad in Ireland, and subsequently in Scotland, ensured that differences between army and parliament were muted initially. From 1649 to 1651, the young Republic was fighting for survival.

In May 1649 the Levellers once more tried to turn the rank and file against the officers. The Levellers had already dissociated themselves from the officers' Agreement and attacked the army leadership for duplicity. They also accused it of seeking to establish a military dictatorship. These attacks led to the arrest, in some cases re-arrest, of the Leveller leaders and their imprisonment in the Tower.[16] The mutiny in the army on their behalf and in support of Leveller aspirations was defeated at Burford. There was a final but very small Leveller mutiny at Oxford in September which was easily put down. The crushing of the Leveller attempts to use the army to realise the movement's own aspirations marked the liquidation of rank-and-file radicalism in the army. In the 1650s the politics of the army were largely politics of the officer corps.

The suppression of the Irish rebellion was undertaken in the summer of 1649 with the departure for Ireland of five horse regiments, including Ireton's and a new double regiment for Cromwell, and ten foot regiments. This meant that two of the army's most capable and astute political members were out of the country on active service. Ireton remained in Ireland as Lord Deputy and acting Commander-in-Chief until his death in November 1651. His stay there and early death deprived the army of one of its most brilliant intellectual and political figures. The conclusion that his 'exile' in Ireland was to some degree self-imposed seems inescapable. In view of the lack of evidence, the reasons for this 'exile' must remain speculative. But Ireton was not trusted by many of the Rumper MPs and this was made all too clear by their rejection of him—and of Harrison too—as a member of the Council of State. It is also possible that he was unhappy, exhausted or even depressed with the turn of events. After all, he must have felt that he had not struggled so long and so hard, especially from 1647, and supported the extreme measures carried out during the revolution of 1648–9 merely to see government fall into the lap of a Rump Parliament which was fast acquiring a taste for power.

Cromwell himself returned triumphant from Ireland at the beginning of May 1650 and was soon leading an army of more than 16,000 officers and men in an invasion of Scotland. Cromwell was fast becoming the most powerful man in the army. Fairfax resigned his commission in June because of scruples about the Scottish invasion. He had also refused to take the Engagement, an oath of loyalty to the Commonwealth. Cromwell as the new Commander-in-Chief won two impressive victories at Dunbar on 3 September 1650 and at Worcester on the same day a year later, thereby dashing the hopes of Prince Charles to gain the English throne. The army thus succeeded in establishing control of the three nations for the parliament and it was to play a central role in guaranteeing that control for successive Interregnum governments. A strong military presence was to remain in both Ireland and Scotland until the Restoration.

The departure of the regiments for service in these two countries was to have important repercussions on the subsequent political evolution of the army. It meant that for the first time since 1647 there existed important geographical divisions within the army. These divisions undermined the close contacts between the regiments which had been possible from 1647 to 1649 when most regiments were stationed in or near London. Even when they had not been within such close call—as with the forces in Yorkshire and in the north—regular and speedy communications between the regiments had been maintained. These contacts had enabled the army to become such a decisive political force in the first place. The splitting up of the army, which was done for military reasons not political ones, first to Ireland and then to Scotland, with other forces serving abroad later on, meant that the officers in or around London came to assume the leading position in army politics. For most of the 1650s, the forces distant from London tended to follow the lead of their colleagues in the capital. The dividing of the regiments considerably weakened army unity and led to growing political divisions, so much so that the possibility of rival factions within the army taking to the field against one another almost became a reality. Moreover, the presence of large numbers of officers in London absent from their regiments meant that the officers ran the risk of getting out of touch with their men. This further weakened army unity and sapped the army's political strength. By late 1659 rank-and-file morale was so low and its confidence in the officers had evaporated to such an extent that soldiers of the Lambert/Disborowe/Fleetwood faction opposing Monck were reported to have said that 'they will not fight, but will make a ring for their officers to fight in'.[17]

Even while the army was engaged on active service, those officers who remained in London continued to ponder ways to advance reform, and they expected the Rump to respond to their concern. Victory at Worcester meant that for the army there could no longer be any excuse on the part of the Rump for prevarication over the reform agenda. In August 1652 the army, after a vigorous debate among the officers in London, presented a petition to the Rump. It was a toned-down version of the demands which had been made in more forceful language and presented to Cromwell. The petition made a variety of requests. Amongst other things, it called for propagation of the Gospel, abolition of tithes, law reform and a consideration of ending the present parliament and the settling of future ones.[18] Over the course of the next few months relations between the army and the Rump deteriorated seriously as the army increasingly came to doubt the Rump's sincerity and willingness to introduce reform. Attempts to bridge the differences between the two failed and the eventual outcome was the dissolution of the Rump by the army on 20 April 1653.

The immediate cause of the dissolution was a fundamental disagreement between army and parliament over the timing and probably the contents of the bill for a new representative. The traditional view is that Cromwell and the officers dissolved the House because the parliament ignored an informal agreement reached the previous night after discussion between themselves and some of the most influential MPs not to proceed with the bill, and instead attempted to pass a bill which included provisions for the House to recruit itself and thus perpetuate itself.[19] This view has been challenged. It is alleged that the cause of the dissolution was the House's resolution to proceed with the bill, but that this bill was for fresh elections not for the recruitment of the House.[20] This was as reckless as it was provocative. New elections would have opened the door not only to the purged members but to men seeking to overthrow the revolution of 1648–9, possibly even a restoration of the Stuarts. Unfortunately, the bill itself has not survived and in its absence there can be no definite answer to the question of what its contents were. What we can be sure of, is that on the night of 19 and 20 April there was a dramatic and decisive change in the relations between the Rump and officers, and that the latter, and Cromwell in particular, felt that the reneging on the agreement of that night was yet another manifestation of the Rump's bad faith. This was the last straw. The officers' patience was exhausted, and they decided that it was time to end the Rump.

The dissolution, as obvious a display of military power as had yet been seen in politics, was spontaneous, although pressure for some sort of action against the Rump had been building up steadily within the army. The army went ahead and dissolved the Rump without really knowing what it was going to replace it with. Thomas Harrison, by now Major-General, favoured the introduction of rule by the Saints, something like a dictatorship of the godly (Barebone's Parliament which eventually succeeded the Rump was a much watered-down version of this), while Lambert favoured strengthening the position of the Council of State, and thus of the executive aspect of government, to provide a counterweight to any future parliament. Some officers, the most notable of whom was Colonel John Okey, had their doubts about the wisdom and legitimacy of the dissolution and soon made them known, but for the majority of the officers the dissolution was an end in itself. Cromwell and his brother-in-law, Colonel John Disborowe (or Desborough), an influential officer in army politics, had been aware of the dangers inherent in a sudden dissolution and of how vulnerable it would make the army to the charge that it was aiming at dictatorship, when they had spoken to the Council of Officers in March. They asked their fellow-officers—and here one hears the voice of Cromwell—what the army would call itself if it dissolved the Rump:

> a state they could not be; They answered that they would call a new Parliament; Then sayes the Generall, the Parliament is not the supreme power, but that is the supreme power that calls it.[21]

This was exactly the point. By dissolving the Rump the army was showing to the world that it held ultimate power in the state. But such a naked display of the sword marked a break with the political strategy that had been pursued since 1647. In that year Major Francis White had been expelled from the General Council for saying that there was no visible power in the land but that of the sword. He had rubbed the rawest of nerves. But the army had been reluctant to accept such a reality and the officers had shied away from its consequences, preferring to co-operate with civilians to achieve its ambitions, hence the limited revolution of 1648–9 and the gradualist approach towards reform. In April 1653 that policy was in ruins, destroyed by the army itself, but not just by the army. In 1649 the army had entrusted civilians with the initiative to implement reform. But the officers had miscalculated badly in assuming a common cause between themselves and the members of the Rump. The stage was set for a conflict between the army, which was anxious to have reforms but unwilling to seize power itself to initiate them, and a parliament truncated by the army, jealous of its rights and privileges, conservative in its aspirations, viewing itself as the nation's authentic political voice and the repository of sovereignty after the abolition of the monarchy and the House of Lords, and, according to some reports, intent on refashioning the army's senior command to make it more amenable to parliamentary control. In the context of 1653 it was obvious which would go under—the Rump. The dissolution did not herald a change of course on the party of the army let alone was it the overture to military rule. At no stage in the 1650s did the army seek to govern by itself. It continued to seek some form of civilian government that would heal the nation's political wounds and provide the solid legal and constitutional foundation on which to build lasting reform. To that extent, the gradualist approach to settlement remained visible amidst the wreckage of the Rump's dissolution.

From April to July 1653 the government was in the hands of the Captain General of the armed forces, Oliver Cromwell, who now emerged as the leading figure in both civilian and military politics, and an interim Council of State consisting of military and civilian personnel —an attempt to blur the appearance of naked military rule. The unity of the army was ensured by the distribution of a declaration on 22 April justifying the dissolution, to which many of the regiments sent back affirmations of support. A few officers expressed doubts openly to Cromwell about the dissolution and one, Captain John Streater, had his dissensions printed, for which he was cashiered. But there appear to have been no resignations over the dissolution. There was much truth in Cromwell's alleged remarks when he returned to the Council of Officers after the dissolution: 'that now they must go hand in hand with him, and justify what was done to the hazard of their lives and Fortunes, as being advised and concurred in it'.[22]

Barebone's Parliament and the establishment of the Protectorate

Cromwell and the officers (almost unanimously) rejected the leftward lunge that Barebone's Parliament seemed to mark. In reality, however, the parliament was far from being the bizarre, extreme sectarian assembly its later reputation has made of it. Most of its members, even if they lacked previous or subsequent parliamentary experience, were drawn from the people who normally sat as MPs at Westminster. Neither in terms of social standing nor general competence and ability were they ill-suited or ill-equipped to perform successfully the task of government. Hard-core religious radicals were in short supply. In comparison with the performance of the Rump or the first Protectorate Parliament, Barebone's applied itself creditably to legislation and to the task of reforming the Commonwealth's finance.[23]

The members of the parliament were chosen by Cromwell and the officers. The selection process was not smooth and took over a month to complete. On 6 June summonses to individuals to sit in the parliament were despatched bearing Cromwell's name as Captain General and Commander-in-Chief. It seems as if it was intended originally to have a measure of self-denial whereby any army officer nominated to the parliament would have laid down his commission.[24] The most likely reason for this was a desire to make the new parliament as civilian a body as possible and for it to be regarded as such. But this idea was abandoned. A few officers were nominated and at the beginning of the session Cromwell, Lambert, Harrison, Disborowe and Mathew Thomlinson were co-opted to serve in the parliament with its approval.

Lambert was far from happy with the creation of Barebone's Parliament, nor with the rebuff to his plea for a stronger Council of State. He played a full part in the interim government between the dissolution of the Rump and the establishment of Barebone's, but when the parliament began to sit he withdrew from the Council of State and by August was reported to have retired to his residence at Wimbledon. However, he did not give up the political fight. Over the next few months he remained active in army affairs, except possibly during a brief sojourn in his native Yorkshire from mid-October to mid-November.[25] Lambert was popular in the army. He had been an able and respected commander during a spell in the north of England from 1647 to 1649, preventing him from playing a direct part in the events surrounding the revolution of 1648–9, and his military achievements in the Scottish campaign of 1650 were noteworthy. Lambert's temporary withdrawal from politics in 1653 was a shrewd move, a tactical retreat to enable a future advance.

As Lambert's stock began to rise, Thomas Harrison's fell. Like his nemesis, he took little part in Barebone's. He withdrew from the Council of State over the summer and fared badly in the elections for the Council in November. But his withdrawal was not an astute move. It was a squandering of political opportunity. By late 1653 the political adeptness which Harrison had displayed in 1647 had disappeared, devoured by his enthusiastic belief in the imminence of the Millenium. There is, of course, the possibility that Harrison and his Fifth Monarchist allies were not so out of touch with reality and that they had concluded that as in December 1647 the only way to counter those in the army and elsewhere that were 'now so full gorged with the flesh of Kings and Nobles, and Captaines, and mighty men, that is with their estates' was by a purge, not of parliament this time, but of the army's senior command. This is improbable.[26] It would also have been unfeasible; this was not 1647. Harrison and his allies were in no position to replicate the Leveller challenge to the grandees in November of that year and Harrison was no Thomas Rainborowe. Reports to the contrary notwithstanding, Harrison did not head a faction within the army. He had no pad from which to launch such a daring coup. By aligning himself with the Saints, Harrison had departed from the political mainstream and, in effect, had committed political suicide. On 21 December he was cashiered from the army. There were a few token resignations of support among the junior officers and some of the soldiers of his regiment in Scotland deserted.

Cromwell was no more enthralled with Barebone's than Lambert or Harrison. From about September 1653 his disappointment with the assembly had given way to distrust. To Cromwell it appeared that the radical members of the parliament were intent on subverting property and removing tithes without providing an alternative source of maintenance for the preaching ministry. If the Rump had appeared too conservative on these issues, Barebone's seemed to be going too far in the opposite direction. The straw that broke the parliament was a report from the committee to examine the appointment and tenure of the clergy and the related question of tithes, matters that struck discordant notes among the proponents of the diversely held views on toleration and property rights within the nation. On 10 December the radicals scored a victory in a division over one of the clauses in the report and two days later the moderate members moved for the parliament's dissolution. The motion was carried, and they proceeded to Whitehall to resign their power to Cromwell. Soldiers, probably acting under orders from Lambert and some other senior officers, but not Cromwell, ensured that the remaining members vacated the chamber.[27] Lambert's political moment had arrived. He had used his sabbatical profitably to mature his thoughts and draft his proposals for constitutional change, the Instrument of Government, a written constitution based on an elected unicameral parliament, a council and a single person, or Lord Protector, which he had ready before Barebone's disappeared.[28]

The Protectorate was established with a minimum of opposition from the army. Exactly how Cromwell was won over is unclear because of a lack of evidence. But he was under pressure even before the dissolution of Barebone's to establish a written constitution which would guarantee 'some solid fundamentals in reference to the state both of religion and politie'.[29] Other officers were won over by what appears to have been a vigorous lobbying campaign in favour of the Instrument by Lambert and his associates, who most likely included officers and civilians. The establishment of the Protectorate, and its acceptance by the army, may seem like a step backwards, but such a conclusion would be wrong. True, the army had been the principal advocate of the trial and execution of Charles I, and it had fought hard and ruthlessly against his eldest son and supporters throughout the British Isles to prevent a restoration of Stuart rule. But in December 1651 Cromwell instigated a meeting with leading Rumpers and a few senior officers to discuss settlement. A proposal that there be something 'monarchical' in any future constitutional arrangements to guarantee a permanent peace was aired. Cromwell thought this might prove 'very effectual', but the officers disagreed.[30] One can understand their revulsion to such an idea, and to the suggestion of placing Charles I's youngest son, the Duke of Gloucester, on the throne, so soon after the crushing of the Stuart cause at Worcester. But two years down the road and after the collapse of another attempt at settlement the political landscape had altered. Hostility to the rule of Charles I did not translate directly into an anathema against the concept of government by a single person, if that person was someone whom the army could trust. Besides, the Heads of the Proposals had sought to limit, not to abolish, the power of Charles and had been supported by most of the officers only to be lost because of the stubborn, uncompromising attitude of the King. A different future was possible to envisage if the man at the head of the government was the army's, the General himself. Such was the extent of Cromwell's prestige, his charisma and the trust and confidence he inspired that his elevation to the Protectorship did not shatter army unity. The acceptance of the title of Lord Protector was one thing, the attempt to substitute the title of King was quite a different matter.

The Protectorate marked a continuation of the limited gradualist revolution embarked upon in 1649. Government was to be largely in the hands of civilians operating within institutions that were not weighted in the army's favour. Cromwell was installed as Lord Protector on 16 December 1653, dressed in 'a plain black suit and cloak',[31] not his army uniform, a conscious public relations ploy to emphasise the non-military character of the new government. But the political presence of the sword could not be disguised that easily. The Protector did not lay down his commission and army officers became members of the Council and sat in the Protectorate Parliament as they had under previous regimes. In modern parlance, the army did not withdraw to barracks.

This exposes two fundamental problems relating to the army that defied resolution during the quest for settlement: how was the army's immense political power to be neutralised, and how was its presence to be accommodated within the existing compass of the state's responsibilities? The Protectorate, especially with Cromwell as head of government and head of the army, went some way towards solving these problems but the arrangement depended too much on Cromwell and his unique relationship with the army based on charisma, trust and shared experience in battle and political struggle. Would the army be satisfied that future Lord Protectors were as suitably qualified to incorporate the two positions and, if not, were not restraints required to ensure that it did not intervene yet again to get its way? Moreover, the arrangement begged the larger question of precisely what was the army's role in the state at a time when it seemed—especially after 1655—increasingly unlikely that it would be called upon to fight another major engagement, at least not in England. There were no precedents for a standing army, let alone one that was so deeply involved in the nation's political life. Was not the defence of England in times of peace better undertaken by the militia forces under the control of local officials whose traditional function it was? The fact that officers sat on the Councils and in the parliaments of the 1650s, including the 'Other House' when it was established, and were active in the civil service, for example in the Post Office or at the Admiralty, meant that military power was institutionalised to some extent. But the officers' presence in these bodies was *ad hoc* and informal and it mocked traditional constitutional and administrative practice. The problem of accommodation, of how to subordinate the military to the state, defied resolution until immediately before the Restoration when the army, under orders from General Monck, deferred to the civilian authorities and made itself the servant of the state, not its hidden master, not even a body that claimed and insisted upon an *ex officio* right to share power with civilians.

Army opposition to the Protectorate

The only serious opposition to the Protectorate from within the army occured in late 1654 and early 1655. This involved two related affairs known as the Three Colonels' Petition and Overton's Plot. The petition, addressed to Cromwell, involved Colonels John Okey, Matthew Alured and Thomas Saunders. The petition itself was drawn up by the former Leveller John Wildman and the drafting had been preceded by meetings involving a number of civilians, mostly former Levellers. The contrivers of the petition hoped to win over and build upon the support of a number of Rumper republican politicians such as John Bradshaw and Sir Arthur Heselrige. The petition claimed that the government established by the Instrument of Government was not legitimate and the petitioners urged the calling of a free and unbound parliament as outlined in the officers' Agreement of 1649.[32]

The appearance of the petition alarmed the government because it occurred at a time when the first Protectorate Parliament was in session and hotly disputing the Instrument in an attempt to revise it in the parliament's favour. The three colonels were arrested. Okey and Alured were court-martialled and Okey was allowed to resign while Alured was cashiered. Both later supported the restored Rump when their colleagues in the Lambert/Disborowe/Fleetwood faction dissolved it in October 1659. Saunders was allowed to resign his commission. Later on he shed his republican sympathies and favoured a restoration of the Stuarts.

Copies of the petition, along with other anti-government tracts, were circulated in Scotland and Ireland. In Scotland a letter signed by various officers at Aberdeen and addressed to Major Abraham Holmes of George Monck's regiment was discovered. The letter called for a conference in Edinburgh to review the present state of affairs and to examine whether the army was able to justify before the Lord its present and past zeal in seeking reform. It transpired that Major General Robert Overton, governor of Hull, had a hand in the letter and had given his tacit approval to the idea of a conference. He was arrested and the opportunity was taken to purge him by the convenient discovery of an alleged plot to seize Monck and march his forces into England. No convincing evidence was produced to support the charge of a plot involving Overton to overthrow the Protectorate. But Overton, who had been under suspicion for some time, remained a prisoner for five years without a trial until he was re-habilitated by the restored Rump in 1659.

The two affairs, related as they were (Overton was present at the discussions preceding the drawing up of the Three Colonels' Petition), were not symptomatic of a more widespread discontent in the army. The Three Colonels' Petition was confined to individuals, as was the discontent in the army in Scotland, which had more to do with conscience rather than a conscious opposition to the Protectorate. The three colonels and their associates had little constructive to offer towards settlement. For them a free parliament was like a shibboleth that would somehow produce a settlement. But free elections in the context of 1654, no less than in April 1653, could easily have resulted in the return of royalists and neuters on the one hand, and uncompromising Republicans on the other, with anarchy as the outcome. The proceedings of the first Protectorate Parliament, which was not a 'free' parliament, of course, should have been a warning to them.

The shallowness of the opposition to the Protectorate centring on the Three Colonels' Petition and Overton's Plot was illustrated in an exchange between Lambert and Lieutenant General Edmund Ludlow in December 1655. Ludlow had served in Ireland as a commissioner and as Lieutenant General of the army there, but had not approved of the establishment of the Protectorate. He was finally recalled from Ireland for distributing the Three Colonels' Petition and other subversive literature. On his return to England he was brought before Cromwell and the Council. Lambert asked him by what authority he felt that he could act against the government. Ludlow replied vaguely that it was on an authority 'equal or superior to this' when he saw that 'the said authority would employ its power for the good of mankind'. Lambert, hitting the nail on the head and exposing the weakness of Ludlow's position, asked who would judge that, 'for all are ready to say they do so, and we ourselves think we use the best of our endeavours to that end', to which Ludlow replied limply that if that was so then their crime was the less.[33] Ludlow had no convincing answer to Lambert's question and for the moment the rest of the officers were prepared to continue supporting Cromwell's government which they judged was making its best endeavours to advance reform and achieve settlement. The army still backed the gradualist approach to reform and Cromwell's policy of healing and settling, evidenced in an official petition from the army presented, perhaps significantly, to Cromwell and not to the parliament in December 1654, reasserting calls for reform but pledging support for the Protector. Secretary Thurloe saw the petition as representing the army's unanimous desire to live and die with Cromwell 'both as their general in military matters, and as their protector in civil'.[34] Thurloe's assessment was good public relations copy and fine as far as it went. But the ties of dependency were not all one way. No matter how uncomfortable Cromwell became with his military persona in the 1650s, he could not slash asunder the umbilical cord that bound him to the army, anymore than the army itself could.

The major-generals

If Cromwell could count on the army not to rock the delicate constitutional structure defined in the Instrument, the same was not true of the parliament. By January 1655 relations between parliament and Protector had reached their nadir. On 20 January the parliament voted that control of the militia, which the Instrument had assigned to the Protector, should be in the hands of the Protector and parliament jointly, a reassertion of the provisions in the Long Parliament's Militia Ordinance of January 1642 and a step along the road to declaring that it should be in parliament alone, an intolerable situation for both Cromwell and the army. For, once the militia had been subjected to parliamentary control, it was obvious that the next target would have been the army itself. The parliament had already made clear its intentions to reduce the army establishment under the popular platform of cost-cutting. Memories of the Rump's ambitions to control the army were still fresh. On 22 January, after five lunar months, Cromwell dissolved the parliament, confident of the army's support. Within a couple of months the army was given a renewed taste of action by putting down Penruddock's rising in favour of Charles Stuart. While the revolt itself was easily suppressed, the greater political crisis, of which the rising was only a symptom, remained as stubbornly intractable as before.

Once again the dissolution of a parliament had provided a quick fix; it still did not resolve the long-term question of settlement. If not quite a coup against the army's own creation, the officers could scarcely paint the latest dissolution in the same rhetorical colours as that of Barebone's, as a repudiation of dangerous fanatics. The Instrument's façade of settlement had fissured even before the foundations had had a chance to settle. Fortunately, or so it appeared, Penruddock's rising had created a diversion. The logical way to counter a military threat was to employ military resources and it was such considerations that gave birth to the 'system' of the major-generals. The major-generals were an expedient devised to tackle the national security fall-out caused by the deep psychological blow that the royalist rising had administered. The institution evolved over the summer and autumn of 1655 and the initiative for it came from the Council, not from the army. But the major-generals and the decimation tax that was to pay for them were serious policy blunders. Never intended to provide a permanent solution to the quest for settlement, let alone marking the first step down the road to a military solution by setting up the Captain General/Lord Protector as the nation's supreme ruler, the major-generals played into the hands of both critics and enemies of the Protectorate and sorely tested the loyalty of its supporters and sympathisers. As with the burden of free quarter in 1647, the major-generals were unpopular and generated a deep vein of resentment that was not confined to the traditional political nation. This is reflected by the negative, oppressive image that persists in folk memory, not all of which can be attributed to the reactionary propaganda of the victorious Restoration regime. It was not just the memory of the military interfering in politics that contributed to the post-Restoration suspicion of a standing army, but the resentment against a particularly repugnant intrusion of the central authority into the localities. Although it was expected that the major-generals would work in unison with the traditional institutions of local power, not usurp their powers, they failed to do so.

In the meantime, the Protectorate had to face a problem that would have been familiar to Charles I: a financial crisis, this one brought about by the cost of the government's ambitious foreign policy against Spain in the West Indies—the Western Design. A conference of the major-generals held in London in May and June 1656 recommended that Cromwell call a new parliament as the best way to end the crisis. The proposal was supported by a majority of the Council, and Cromwell, who along with some of the Council had initially favoured extending the decimation tax to raise money, was won over, swayed no doubt by the major-generals' confidence of being able to secure a parliament favourable to the government. Alas, they overestimated their management skills and a number of MPs opposed to the government were returned. The extent of the major-generals' failure can be grasped from a letter by Thomas Kelsey, Major-General for Kent. On 26 August 1656 he wrote to Cromwell that most of the 'Cavaliers fell in with the Presbyterians against you and the Government, and the spirit is generally bitter against swordsmen, decimators, courtiers, etc., and most of those chosen to sit in the ensuing Parliament are of the same spirit'.[35] In Kent the traditional MPs were returned but Kelsey favoured the imposition of a test on all members before allowing them to sit to ensure that they would not meddle with the Instrument, which he had helped promote in 1653.[36] Such a test was applied and some members were excluded. Nevertheless, a number of MPs who held quite different ideas of settlement from those of the army were returned and took their seats and, no matter the political cost, they were determined to challenge the army and its political pretensions. However, it was not over the place of parliaments in any constitutional settlement that the next major crisis was to erupt, but over something quite unexpected—the question of kingship.

The kingship crisis

Cromwell had been disappointed with his first parliament, possibly with the idea of parliaments *tout court*. In his letter Major Kelsey had assured the Protector that he and his subordinates would stand by Cromwell 'with life and fortune' to maintain 'the interest of God's people, which is to be preferred before 1,000 Parliaments'.[37] After the army's experience with the Rump, Barebone's and the first Protectorate Parliament, such an outpouring of frustration and disillusionment with the parliamentary process is understandable. But is is astonishingly vague and politically naive. Cromwell himself knew better. A division of opinion over how to define 'the interest of God's people' had caused the war in 1642. Even with the spilling of such much blood the wounds remained unhealed and in the interim further rifts had opened. The imposition of a military settlement, the implication of Kelsey's statement, held no appeal for Cromwell. Nor was it a plausible solution. In many ways Cromwell remained a plain country squire. He was unsuited by temperament and ambition to become a dictator. To do so would have meant the disavowal of much of the country ethos, the decent values he still held dear. It is not surprising that he was won over to the idea of calling a new parliament. Besides, he had little option.

As the session progressed, Cromwell was impressed by the members' attempts to devise proposals for settlement and by what appeared to be the parliament's positive attitude towards the Protector.[38] This does not mean that the House met in September 1656 armed with blueprints for reform nor with the necessary consensus to achieve it. As was so often the case in the 1650s, the proposals evolved in response to a crisis, this time the case of James Naylor, the Quaker who entered Bristol on the back of a horse in the manner of Christ's entry into Jerusalem. He was brought before the House on a charge of blasphemy. Naylor's case exposed a major source of contention unaddressed by the Instrument. Who was to arbitrate between parliament and Protector if the two disagreed? The proposals for settlement which emerged from the controversy surrounding Naylor's case became known as the Humble Petition and Advice. As first presented, they included the offer of kingship. Here at last the tantalising prospect of an enduring settlement, especially as it was the work of civilians, was laid before Cromwell. But to accept it in full Cromwell would have alienated large sections of the army; even by accepting it without the kingship clause, he was straining the loyalty of many officers who had followed him through the twists and turns of the 1650s.

The prospect of a House of Cromwell became such a major crisis and marked a turning point in the politics of the 1650s for a number of reasons. Firstly, the crisis represented a civilian/military conflict, but with divisions that cut across both groups as well. Secondly, the Humble Petition and Advice marked the first promising attempt at settlement to emerge from civilians. But, in the light of their experience with civilian politicians since 1647, the officers, although obviously not all, were suspicious of the proposals to tamper with the Instrument emanating from this quarter. Suspicion was fuelled by insecurity, and compounded by doubts about the motivation of the civilian promoters of the Humble Petition. Given the ambitions of the previous parliament, and before that the Rump, there was no doubt that civilians preferred the army to withdraw from politics and that given the opportunity they would legislate to that end. Could the self-proclaimed champions and guardians of the people's rights allow themselves to abdicate their responsibilities and simply fade away without any assurance that those rights would be guaranteed? The answer was obvious: the army had stood resolute in the spring of 1647; it should do so again. Unfortunately the army had nothing to offer as a remedy for the Instrument's shortcomings. It had reached the limits of its creativity. Its officers no longer acted as a think-tank, hatching and nurturing constitutional plans for settlement. From a civilian perspective, it had become an impediment to progress, an anachronism in politics. Thirdly, unless resolved, the crisis made a split within the army not only possible but probable. It marked the most serious threat to unity since the division over the Irish service in 1647. This threat was exacerbated by the fact that it existed at the centre, not on the periphery in Ireland or Scotland where it could have been contained. If unity cracked at the centre, as was to happen within the next two years, the army would implode as a political force. Fourthly, there was a danger of a rift between Cromwell and his officers. Opposition to kingship ran deep among them. Cromwell was unable to run the risk of an appeal over the heads of the anti-kingship officers in an attempt to build a new power base. Nor could he hope to carry out 'a night of the long knives' and cashier a few senior officers as an example and chart his own course. Sir Charles Firth remarked that 'the officers were the representatives of Cromwell's party; the army was the constituency Cromwell represented'.[39] If so, it was a constituency that held him captive, and one from which he could not break free without running the risk of self-destruction. This was part of the unenviable legacy that he left his son and it stalked all successive regimes until the army itself ceased to function as a political force. Obversely, there was no individual of substance within the army strong enough to challenge Cromwell's ascendancy.

The Cromwellian project of healing and settling had begun to unravel.

The end of Oliver Cromwell's Protectorate

Cromwell rejected the offer of kingship and on 26 June 1657 he was installed for a second time as Lord Protector in a ceremony far more pompous than the previous one, and with a more obviously civilian entourage accompanying him. The political controversy did not stop with his refusal of kingship, and supporters and opponents of kingship continued to provoke each other. However, the coalition of anti-kingship officers began to break up. The chief loser from this was John Lambert. He used every opportunity to show his prejudice against the Humble Petition, but did not go so far as to oppose it root and branch. By early July he had isolated himself within the army, and Cromwell was able to purge him with no overt response in his favour from his colleagues. Why was this so? The answer must lie in the fact that during the kingship crisis although there was a lot of revulsion in the army against the title of king, which finally forced Cromwell to reject it, there was also a substantial middle ground among the officers, consisting of men who opposed the title, but who were still prepared to follow Cromwell and the policy of healing and settling once that divisive issue had been laid aside. The middle ground was probably made up of officers who supported Cromwell for reasons that included loyalty and genuine belief that the fact of settlement and reform was bound up inseparably with that of the Protector. At a more mundane level, their own self-interest, especially as beneficiaries from the sales of crown lands, must have figured as well. Only the rule of law and a universally recognised administration of justice could ensure that their purchases remained legally valid. They probably concluded that the best way to guarantee this was to stick with Cromwell. Lambert miscalculated and under-estimated the strength of this middle ground; Charles Fleetwood and John Disborowe, the other two key members of the army, probably subscribed to aspects of it, hence their desire to see the new constitution work. However, Lambert's downfall swelled the ranks of former officers with the most substantial figure of all.

Neither the Humble Petition, with its provision for 'the Other House' which could, if need be, act as a buffer between the Protector and the elected chamber, nor the second session of the parliament, beginning on 20 January 1658, provided the country with settlement. Within two weeks the parliament had been dissolved by the Protector. There was a bitter dispute in the Commons about how to style 'the Other House', while Rumper republicans like Sir Arthur Hesilrige and Thomas Scott tried to wreck the entire proceedings. There was also an attempt to stir up disaffection in the army with a petition in favour of restoring the Rump. This led to the cashiering of six officers of Cromwell's regiment, including the Major. But the rest of the army remained firmly behind him.

The future became even more uncertain over the next few months in view of the Protector's deteriorating health. By the end of August when Cromwell was in his death struggle, there are indications that the army officers were at last waking up to the likelihood of his demise and were trying to prepare themselves by staking out positions in anticipation of the immense political vacuum that would ensue. Army unity remained fragile. Signs of the future division between Protectorian and anti-Protectorian officers, the latter centring on Fleetwood's residence at Wallingford House, emerged and a number of junior officers around London emerged as an important caucus and remained so until the restoration of the Rump in 1659, but they were never more than a pressure group. Cromwell's son Henry, who was serving in Ireland as Lord Deputy, portrayed the situation vividly in a letter to Thurloe at the end of June:

> Have you any settlement? Does not your peace depend upon his highness's life, and upon his peculiar skill, and faculty and personall interest in the army as now modelled and commanded? I say, beneath the immediate hand of God (if I know anything of the affaires in England) there is no other reason why wee are not in blood at this day.[40]

Allowing for some obvious exaggeration, especially in the last part of the statement, it was quite a shrewd assessment of affairs at the end of Oliver Cromwell's Protectorate.

After the death of Cromwell, the army had few reservations to try to win back some of the political ground it felt that it had lost during the last eighteen months or so. Whatever qualms the officers had had about challenging Cromwell, they had few regarding his son and successor, Richard.

In an address presented to Richard on 18 September, shortly after his father's death, the officers wrote their own epitaph for Oliver declaring that he had considered the army 'the choicest Saints, his chiefest Worthies'. They urged the new Protector to ensure that the new Privy Council (the Humble Petition and the Additional Petition and Advise reverted to the style 'Privy Council' instead of Council of State under the Rump, or simply Council as under the Instrument) was composed of men 'of known Godliness, and sober Principles' and 'that they with your Highness and your Army' should carry on the work of reform.[41] The officers were advocating a kind of tripartite government of Protector, Privy Council and army as the ideal solution to the problem of settlement. It was a bold claim and went much further, and was put in much stronger language, than anything that had been tendered to the army. The army dropped pretences. The officers now claimed unambiguously that they were a separate estate, a new departure in English constitutional history and one wholly conflicting with the civilians' agenda. But the address marked the beginnings of serious divisions within the army. In Ireland Henry Cromwell had a different address of loyalty drawn up and sent it for subscription throughout the army there. In Scotland Monck was not quite so independent as Henry, despite the fact that the two men appear to have corresponded with each other. Fleetwood forwarded the army's address to Monck requesting that the officers in Scotland sign it. Monck had already set in motion his own address but in the end dropped it in favour of the address sent from London. However, he sent a copy of the address he had originally intended to Thurloe, presumably to show that he was prepared to maintain his independence. Army unity could no longer be taken for granted. Ironically the army had succeeded where Charles I had failed, in imposing unity on the three kingdoms, but in so doing it had divided itself, fatally.

The chaos of 1659

National politics from late 1658 to April 1660 have parallels with those between March 1647 and January 1649. Both periods are marked by great fluidity and constantly shifting alignments. But in terms of army politics there was a difference. In the earlier period there had been a consistency in the army policy and, more important, there had been firm and decisive leadership. In the later period these factors were lacking. The army itself was not creating programmes for settlement as it had done for example with the Heads of the Proposals in 1647, the Remonstrance of 1648, or the officers' Agreement of 1649. There does not appear to have been the same high quality of political debate as had been manifested, for example, at Reading or Putney in 1647 or at Whitehall in 1649. Nor was there the same level of political consciousness running throughout the army as before. For the most part the rank and file were apathetic towards events by the end of the 1650s. The army still showed itself responsive to some of the most innovative political ideas of the day—for example, Harrington's idea of a select senate—but those ideas were no longer being developed and refined within the army's own ranks by men of the calibre of Ireton or the young Lambert, and even if they had been, there was no one with the political skills of Cromwell to try to put them into practice. The army had no clear idea of its political direction in the late 1650s. First it tried to see how far it could go with Richard Cromwell, and eventually got rid of him. Then it recalled the Rump, failing to realise the extent of the ambitions and passionately held convictions about parliamentary supremacy of men like Heselrige and Thomas Scott. It got rid of the Rump. Then it flirted with Harringtonian notions. Gradually force came to be used as an end in itself. The army lost the ability to differentiate between the creative use of force, of 'right and might well met' (the military interventions in 1647, the revolution of 1648–9, the dissolution of the Rump and the dissolution of Barebone's, in all of which the power of the sword had been used to help set up an alternative, and what was hoped viable, route to settlement), and its uncreative use. After 1657 the army stumbled from one prop to another—Protector, Rump, Committee of Safety, Army Council—seeking some kind of crutch that could give government and the army's intervention an appearance of legitimacy. Insofar as the army still searched for legitimacy, there was consistency with the political role it had inherited from 1647–9; the officers did not want to rule as a military dictatorship.

From the end of 1658 onwards, the tensions within the army already present at the time of Oliver's death became unmanageable and the army tore itself and the Good Old Cause to pieces. There was a split between Protectorian and anti-Protectorian officers in April 1659, between officers loyal to the restored Rump and those opposed to its claims to be the source of military authority (the Lambert/Disborowe/Fleetwood faction) in October, and finally and decisively between the Lambert/Disborowe/Fleetwood faction and the army in Scotland. It was during this last episode, from October to December 1659, that the army's political role as it had existed for the previous twelve years really ceased.

The Lambert/Disborowe/Fleetwood faction, claiming to speak for the whole army, envisaged a General Council of the Army to decide the nation's future government. But in reality the faction could not claim to be representative of much beyond itself. It did not represent all of its fellow officers, it did not represent the soldiery, who were to be excluded from the Council, and it most certainly did not represent any significant element of the political nation. The faction's constituency was limited to its members and a small band of civilians. The contrast with 1647–9 is obvious. If it was a fag-end of the Long Parliament which legitimised the revolution of 1648–9, it was a fag-end of the army which attempted to further that revolution in late 1659. Faced with opposition from Monck in Scotland and from units declaring for the Rump, the faction's toehold on power gave way and the Rump was re-restored towards the end of December.

The army and the Restoration

With the return of the Rump, the politics of the army were transformed. This was less the result of policies introduced by the Rump, such as a new round of purges, and more a consequence of the emergence of Monck as the most powerful man in the army and, after his arrival in London in the new year, the most powerful man in the country. Under Monck's leadership the army renounced its claim to be the guardian of the Good Old Cause, and for the first time in thirteen years was prepared to hand over power unconditionally to civilians who were to be given a blank cheque to decide what sort of government they wanted, even if it was obvious that this would mean the readmission of the MPs purged by Colonel Pride in 1648 and the return of the 'common enemy', 'the King of Scots', 'the pretended king', Charles Stuart.

This did not come about easily, nor was it predetermined, least of all by Monck when he began his march south on 1 January 1660, but arguably it was what the majority of the country wanted. Under Monck, the army acquiesced in its own political emasculation, despite unco-ordinated resistance from some serving officers and purged officers. The acquiescence of the army is not surprising. By the beginning of 1660, with the exception of Monck's forces which he had purged while still in Scotland, replacing officers commissioned by the Rump over the summer with men loyal to him, and the forces in Ireland who were under the command of men sympathising with Monck after a coup against Dublin Castle in December, the army was broken and dispirited. The *esprit* of the officer corps was shattered, a result of the purges by the Rump over the summer of 1659, by the Lambert/Disborowe/Fleetwood faction after the October coup, and by the Rump again in January 1660. Monck compounded this by ensuring that when he came to London the regiments accompanying him were quartered there. Most of those already in the City were ordered to leave the capital for quarters elsewhere, but not within easy distance of each other. The object was to reduce the possibility of communications between them as in 1647.[42] The credibility of the officers in the eyes of the nation, and in the eyes of fellow-adherents of the Good Old Cause, had been destroyed anyway by the events of the previous few months, and their pretensions to be the guardians of that Cause, let alone the vanguard to further it, were shattered. By April 1660, after some further purging, Monck and his closest advisers decided that a clear statement from the army indicating that it would obey a decision made by the civilian authorities was needed. This took the form of a declaration from the regiments to which subscriptions were required, in some cases under threat of dismissal, to obey all commands of Monck, the Council of State and whatever the new parliament (the Convention Parliament) would determine. In the declaration the army also pledged itself not to meddle in affairs of state on the grounds that it thereby made itself a divided interest from the rest of the people.[43] In 1647 the army had claimed that it was not a divided interest, not a mercenary army, but a body of citizens in arms. This claim was the army's *raison d'être* for its political role in the 1650s. In 1660 the claim was being turned on its head. Instead of being employed to justify an active political role it was made to renounce such a role and to justify the army's subservience and subordination to civilian government.

The declaration was presented to Monck on 9 April, by which time it was obvious that a restoration of the Stuarts was just around the corner. Lambert's last hurrah in April, an unsuccessful rising to salvage whatever from the detritus of the Good Old Cause, fizzled out almost as farce. The historical tide had turned decisively. On 2 May the officers declared their willingness to accept the Declaration of Breda in an Address which was forwarded to the new king. Subscriptions to the Address from those regiments not in London soon followed, and on 23 May Charles II arrived in London.

Conclusion

Socially and economically, many of the senior officers were members of the traditional ruling class. Most did not belong to the upper echelons of their class, but they were men of some standing in their immediate localities, although not necessarily in their counties. They are best described in Professor Everitt's words: 'They shone instead as lesser stars in the larger constellations of *county* gentry . . .'[44] The senior officers tended to have been educated formally (usually at one or other of the universities and at one of the Inns of Court) or had entered a trade. Some were younger sons. This was the sort of background of men like Henry Ireton, John Lambert, William Sydenham, Robert Lilburne, Thomas Saunders, Matthew Alured, Edward Whalley, William Goffe (son of a rector), John Jones and John Disborowe, although not all were younger sons (e.g. Ireton, Lambert, Lilburne and Sydenham). These names span a wide spectrum of political opinion and allegiance among the officers in the 1650s. They were not the sort of men who emerged as leading figures in their localities and as MPs soon after 1640, men like Sir William Brereton in Cheshire or John Pyne in Somerset, or even Oliver Cromwell himself. There is a definite sense in which it was only the war and their subsequent army careers which made these men politically important. One can envisage a talented man like Ireton or Lambert playing a leading role in local or even national politics in virtually any circumstances, but it is difficult to see how a Robert Lilburne, a Thomas Saunders, a Matthew Alured, a John Jones or even a John Disborowe would have reached such positions of power without the civil war and their military careers (and in the case of Disborowe, without his family ties with Cromwell).[45] Even some of those who did not come from this background—and it must be remembered that in the army promotion usually depended upon merit—such as John Okey, in origin probably a substantial citizen of London, soon showed that they shared its style and aspirations. The argument that it was the war that helped establish and further the political careers of most of the officers applies to such men as well.

The officers were also affected by what David Underdown has characterised as a conflict between 'two contradictory elements, one moderate and reformist, the other radical and revolutionary' which influenced many members of the traditional ruling class and their attitudes and reactions to events during the Revolution.[46] Intellectually the officers also shared with many of their contemporaries what J. G. A. Pocock has described as 'the dilemma of Cromwellian Puritanism . . . a dilemma between several modes of action'.[47] Their background and their investment in crown lands gave many senior, and junior, officers a tendency to share in some of the accepted assumptions about the established social and economic order. This inhibited their revolutionary ardour. The question of law reform, which remained one of the consistent demands of the army, provides a good illustration of this. Would not too radical a reform of the laws have endangered the officers' own social position and in many cases their newly acquired wealth? The officers needed a comprehensive legal framework legitimised by a constitution acceptable to the majority of the political nation as much as any other landholders to secure their social standing. They were, as a result, uneasy about casting their fate and fortune to the winds of profound revolutionary social change. The officers were incapable of ensuring the execution of a policy of fundamental reform of the courts and property laws which according to one distinguished contemporary, Sir Mathew Hale, would have made a Restoration more difficult to achieve.[48] Nor were they capable of giving the necessary leadership to the second component of what Professor Conrad Russell has called the 'alliance' or 'union between the discontents of the Parliamentary gentry and those of their social inferiors'—an alliance based on Puritanism and resentment of arbitrary taxation which had helped to cause the civil war in the first place.[49] If the officers had been willing to provide leadership to these 'social inferiors', then what Russell calls the second of the two revolutions within the English Revolution, the revolution of 1647–9, 'the revolution of the army', would have been more thoroughgoing.[50]

In an age which lacked political parties, the army came close to being one. But it lacked a true political identity, whether it was reformist/gradualist or radical/revolutionary. By and large it tended towards the former. This crisis of identity ran deep and its implications were more important not just for army politics but for the English Revolution as a whole. Was the army, and in particular its officers who shaped its policy virtually alone from late 1647, to pursue a moderate or limited revolution or a radical one? Were the officers to proceed cautiously along the road to reform, or risk all, especially their gains from the sales of crown lands, by pursuing a fully fledged revolutionary policy which could have brought about a social revolution the consequences of which they feared? Their inability to make up their minds about this lies at the root of the army's politics. It was a tragic flaw which led to the chaos of 1659 and ultimately to the downfall of the Good Old Cause.

An army made the revolution of 1648–9; it also made the Restoration of May 1660. But it was not really the army of 1647–59 which brought about the latter development. It was the force under Monck, a man keen on discipline who surrounded himself by officers of like mind. Neither Monck nor his fellow-officers shared this identity crisis. They had resolved it, perhaps it had never really troubled them. For them the army ought to be subservient to the civilian authorities. It was this belief plus the divisions, incompetence and confusion that prevailed among the Lambert/Disborowe/Fleetwood faction which helped make the army's contribution to the Restoration so decisive, and it was this belief that the army continued to uphold after it.

Notes

1. The feasibility of settlement and the problems in the way receive a well-balanced analysis in the editor's Introduction to G. E. Aylmer (ed.), *The Interregnum: The Quest for Settlement 1646–1660* (London, 1972).
2. See for example C. H. Firth, *Cromwell's Army* (London 1962 edition), pp. 31–3.
3. M. Kishlansky, *The Rise of the New Model Army*, (Cambridge, 1980), pp. 11–15, 26–51, esp pp. 37–47; idem, 'The Case of the Army Truly Stated: The Creation of the New Model Army', *Past and Present*, 81 (1978), pp. 51–74. See also J. S. Morrill, *The Revolt of the Provinces* (London, 1976), pp. 62–3.
4. A. Woolrych, *Soldiers and Statesmen* (Oxford, 1987), pp. 16–23; I. Gentles, *The New Model Army* (Oxford, 1992), pp. 1–27, esp pp. 16–21.
5. Regrettably, the view of those who were conscripted, and such men formed the bulk of the forces on both sides, will never be known. However, it cannot be assumed that just because they have left no record of their preferences, the impressed were, therefore, apolitical. Besides, for better or worse, politics is energised and given momentum by those who are actively committed to particular causes. On recruitment to the New Model see ibid, pp 31–40, esp p. 40.
6. For the background to parliamentary politics at this time and for an analysis of the terms 'Presbyterian peace party', 'Independent' and 'middle group', which still remain the categories making most sense of alignments in the Commons, see D. Underdown, *Pride's Purge* (Oxford, 1971). Cf. M. Kishlansky, *The Rise of the New Model Army* (Cambridge, 1979). Less satisfactory is J. R. MacCormack, *Revolutionary Politics in the Long Parliament* (Cambridge, Mass, 1973).
7. The *Declaration* is reprinted in part in J. P. Kenyon (ed.), *The Stuart Constitution* (Cambridge, 1966), p. 296.
8. The Heads of the Proposals are reprinted in S. R. Gardiner (ed.), *Constitutional Documents of the Puritan Revolution*, 3rd edn (Oxford, 1906), pp. 316–26. But cf. J. S. A. Adamson, 'The English Nobility and the Projected Settlement of 1647', *Historical Journal*, 30 (1987), pp. 571–2, for the view that Ireton was not the author but only drafted the Heads on behalf of Viscount Say and Sele, Lord Wharton and possibly Sir Henry Vane. See also Woolrych, *Soldiers and Statesmen*, p. 152; Gentles, *New Model Army*, p. 182.
9. British Library E 413 (17), *The Copy of a Letter to his Excellency Sir Thomas Fairfax*.
10. The Solemn Engagement is reprinted in J. Rushworth, *Historical Collections*, 7 vols (1659–1701), Vol. vi, pp. 510–12.

11. *A Remonstrance sent from Colonel Lilburne's Regiment to his Excellency Sir Thomas Fairfax*, reprinted in Rushworth, *Historical Collections*, Vol. vii, pp. 913–14.
12. Kenyon, *The Stuart Constitution*, pp. 318–19.
13. *Historical Manuscripts Commission Duke of Buccleuch and Queensbury at Montagu House*, Vol. i, p. 309.
14. The officers' Agreement is reprinted in D. M. Wolfe (ed.), *Leveller Manifestoes of the Puritan Revolution* (N. Y., 1867), pp. 333–54.
15. C. H. Firth (ed.), *The Clarke Papers*, 4 vols (Camden Society, 1891–1901), Vol. ii, pp. 175–86, passim.
16. For Leveller attacks on the army leadership see *England's New Chains Discovered* and *The Second Part of England's New Chains Discovered* reprinted in W. Haller and G. Davies (eds), *The Leveller Tracts, 1647–1653* (Gloucester, Mass, 1964), pp. 157–70, 172–89; *The Hunting of the Foxes*, reprinted in Wolfe, *Leveller Manifestoes*, pp. 359–83.
17. *Clarke Papers*, Vol. iv, p. 300.
18. *Journal of the House of Commons*, Vol. viii, pp. 164–5.
19. S. R. Gardiner, *History of the Commonwealth and Protectorate*, 4 vols (London, 1903), Vol. ii, pp. 251–65 provides a classic illustration of this view.
20. B. Worden, *The Rump Parliament* (Cambridge, 1974), pp. 337, 338, 365–6, 373, 377; A. Woolrych, *Commonwealth to Protectorate* (Oxford, 1982), chapters 2 and 3.
21. C. H. Firth, 'Cromwell and the Expulsion of the Long Parliament in 1653', *English Historical Review*, 8 (1893), p. 528.
22. J. Heath, *Flagellum* (1679), p. 128.
23. Woolrych, *Commonwealth to Protectorate*, chapters 6 and 7 passim, pp. 236–7, 291–2, 332–3.
24. *Clarke Papers*, Vol. iii, pp. 4, 7.
25. C[alendar of] S[tate] P[apers] D[omestic] *1652–1653*, pp. 332, 341, 342, 377, 387, 395, 410, 421, 451;). O. Ogle, W. H. Bliss and W. D. Macray (eds), *Calendar of the Clarendon State Papers*, Vol. ii, pp. 205–6, 246; *C. S. P. Venice 1653–1654*, pp. 124–5; C. H. Firth (ed.), *Scotland and the Commonwealth* (Scottish History Society, xviii, 1895), p. 238; T. Birch (ed.), *State Papers of John Thurloe*, 7 vols, 1762), Vol. i, p. 393; Woolrych, *Commonwealth to Protectorate*, pp. 277, 353–4.
26. See B. S. Capp, *The Fifth Monarchy Men* (London, 1972), pp. 66, 71; Woolrych, *Commonwealth to Protectorate*, pp. 330–2. The quotation is from William Dell, *The Trydale of Spirits* (London 1653), cited in ibid., p. 331.
27. Woolrych, *Commonwealth to Protectorate*, pp. 335–9, 345–7.
28. The Instrument of Government is reprinted in Gardiner, *Constitutional Documents*, pp. 405–17.

29. *Thurloe State Papers*, Vol. i, pp. 591–2.
30. Bulstrode Whitelocke, *Memorials of the English Affairs* (London, 1732), pp. 516–17; B. Worden, *The Rump Parliament* (Cambridge, 1974), pp. 276–7; Woolrych, *Commonwealth to Protectorate*, pp. 29–31.
31. *Thurloe State Papers*, Vol. i, p. 632.
32. The petition is calendared in the *C. S. P. D. 1653–54*, pp. 302–4 under 1653 instead of 1654.
33. C. H. Firth (ed.), *Memoirs of Edmund Ludlow*, 2 vols (Oxford, 1894), Vol. i, pp. 434–6.
34. R. Vaughan, *The Protectorate of Oliver Cromwell*, 2 vols (1879), Vol. i, 87–8.
35. *C. S. P. D. 1656–1657*, p. 87.
36. Ibid., pp 87–8; A. Everitt, *The Community of Kent and the Great Rebellion 1640–60* (Leicester, 1966), pp. 294–5. Cf. *H. M. C. Portland*, Vol. iii, p. 208.
37. *C. S. P. D. 1656–1657*, p. 88.
38. Cf. Professor Underdown's argument that by 1657 many of the older families in the counties were beginning to accept the Protectorate and to return to active politics and that therefore the parliament made a more positive contribution to the problem of settlement (D. Underdown, 'Settlement in the Counties 1653–1658', in Aylmer (ed.), *The Interregnum*, p. 177).
39. C. H. Firth, *The Last Years of the Protectorate*, 2 vols (Oxford, 1909), Vol. i, p. 138. For a different view see H. R. Trevor-Roper, 'Oliver Cromwell and his Parliaments', in *Religion, the Reformation and Social Change*, 2nd edn (London, 1972), pp. 345–91, esp. p. 384.
40. *Thurloe State Papers*, Vol. i, p. 218.
41. The address is reprinted in *The Old Parliamentary or Constitutional History of England*, 24 vols, 2nd edn (1761–3), Vol. xxi, pp. 233–6.
42. Monck purged three-eighths of the officer corps after his arrival. Attrition was especially high among the junior officers, with two-thirds of the captains losing their commands. See R. Hutton, *The Restoration* (Oxford, 1985), p. 85 citing H. Reece, 'The Military Presence in England 1649–1660', unpublished University of Oxford D. Phil., 1981, pp. 266–8.
43. The declaration is printed in Sir Richard Baker, *A Chronicle of the Kings and Queens of England*, continued by Edward Phillips (1684), p. 697.
44. Everitt, *Community of Kent*, p. 34. Cf. G. E. Aylmer, *The State's Servants* (London, 1973), p. 328.
45. It should of course be remembered that Fleetwood, Richard Ingoldsby and John Reynolds came from country gentry backgrounds, but they were also younger sons. Fleetwood and Ingoldsby were also related to Cromwell.
46. Underdown, *Pride's Purge*, pp. 8, 353.
47. J. G. A. Pocock, *The Machiavellian Moment* (Princeton, N. J., 1975), p. 338.

48. M. Hale, *Some Considerations Touching the Alteration of Laws*, quoted in D. Veall, *The Popular Movement for Law Reform 1640–1660* (Oxford, 1970), pp. 228–9.
49. C. Russell (ed.), *The Origins of the English Civil War* (London 1973), p. 27.
50. Ibid., p. 3. Professor Russell's notion of the two revolutions echoes but is not the same as Dr Hill's concept of the two revolutions in the mid-seventeenth century (C. Hill, *The World Turned Upside Down* (London, 1973), p. 12). For the reasons given above, the army was not able to ensure the success of Dr Hill's second revolution (the establishment of communal property, more democracy in politics and law, etc.).

Further Reading

Union and Disunion in the British Isles 1637–1660

The books and articles cited in the chapter notes contain copious reference to works worth following up. Here is a selection of some additional items (arranged alphabetically) on themes which continue to stimulate serious study.

BOOKS

R. Ash (ed.), *Three Nations—A Common History? England, Scotland, Ireland and British History* (Bochum, 1993); B. Barilyn and P. O. Morgan (eds), *Strangers with the Realm: Cultural Margins of the First British Empire* (Chapel Hill and London, 1991); B. Bradshaw, A. Hadfield and W. Maley (eds), *Representing Ireland: Literature and the Origins of Conflict, 1634–1660* (Cambridge, 1993); C. Brady and R. Gillespie (eds), *Natives and Newcomers: Essays on the making of Irish Colonial Society, 1534–1641* (Dublin, 1986); K. M. Brown, *Kingdom or Province: Scotland and the Regal Union* (London, 1992); N. Canny, *From Reformation to Restoration: Ireland, 1534–1660* (Dublin, 1987); N. Canny and P. Pagden (eds), *Colonial Identity in the Atlantic World, 1500–1800* (Princeton, 1987); S. G. Ellis and S. Barber (eds), *Conquest and Union: Fashioning a British State, 1485–1725* (London, 1995); A. Grant and K. J. Sturges (eds), *Uniting the Kingdom* (London, 1995); R. Hutton, *The British Republic, 1649–60* (London, 1990); H. F. Kearney, *Strafford in Ireland*, 2nd edn (Cambridge, 1989); B. P. Levack, *The Formation of the British State: England, Scotland and the Union, 1603–1707* (Oxford, 1991); R. Mason (ed.), *Scots and Britons: Scottish Political Thought and the Union of 1603* (Cambridge, 1994); J. S.

Morrill (ed.), *The Scottish National Covenant in its British Context* (Edinburgh, 1991); J. H. Ohlmeyer, *Civil War and Restoration in the Three Kingdoms: The Career of Randall MacDonnell, Earl of Antrim* (Cambridge, 1993); H. Perceval-Maxwell, *The Outbreak of the Irish Rebellion of 1641* (Dublin, 1994); C. Russell, *The Causes of the English Civil War* (Oxford 1990) and *The Fall of the British Monarchies* (Oxford, 1991); D. Stevenson, *Union, Revolution and Religion in Seventeenth-Century Scotland* (London, 1997), (collected articles); G. Williams, *When was Wales?* (London, 1985).

ARTICLES

D. Armitage, 'The Cromwellian Protectorate and the Language of Empire', *Historical Journal*, 35 (1992); T. G. Barnard, 'Crisis of Identity Among Irish Protestants, 1641–1685', *Past and Present*, 129 (1990), and 'Irish Images of Cromwell' in R. C. Richardson (ed.), *Images of Oliver Cromwell* (Manchester, 1993); J. Buckroyd, 'Bridging the Gap: Scotland 1659–1660', *Scottish Historical Review*, 1987); D. Cannadine, 'British History—Past, Present—and Future?', *Past and Present*, 116 (1987); L. Colley, 'Britishness and Otherness: An Argument', *Journal of British Studies*, 31 (1992); S. Ellis, ' "Not mere English": The British Perspective, 1400–1650', *History Today*, 38 (1988); J. H. Elliott, 'A Europe of Composite Monarchies', *Past and Present*, 137 (1992); J. S. Morrill, 'A British Patriarchy? Ecclesiastical Imperialism under the Early Stuarts' in A. Fletcher and P. Roberts (eds), *Religion, Culture and Society in Early Modern Britain* (London, 1994); H. Perceval-Maxwell, 'Ireland and the Monarchy in the Early Stuart Kingdom', *Historical Journal*, 34 (1991); C. Russell, 'The British Problem and the English Civil War', *History*, 72 (1987), and 'The British Background to the Irish Rebellion of 1641', *Historical Research*, 61 (1988); J. Wormald, 'The Creation of Britain; Multiple Kingdoms of Core and Colonies?', *Transactions of the Royal Historical Society*, 6th series, 2 (1992).

Religion, Politics and Welshness, 1649–1660

The following list of suggestions for further reading concentrates almost exclusively on titles in the English language. Some works in Welsh are recommended where there is no obvious English alternative. It should be noted, however, that there is an extensive literature in Welsh, particularly on the topics of religion and culture, which extends very considerably what is readily available to the student of Interregnum Wales.

A good launching point for the history of Wales in general might be Philip Jenkins, *A History of Modern Wales 1536–1990* (Cardiff, 1992), but the most accessible detailed treatment of the early modern period would be the two volumes in the Oxford University Press History of Wales series: G. Williams, *Recovery, Reorientation and Reformation. Wales c.1415–1642* (Oxford, 1987) and G. H. Jenkins, *The Foundations of Modern Wales 1642–1780* (Oxford, 1987). The latter contains two very substantial chapters on the Interregnum, and a very full bibliography. There is a great deal of lasting value in A. H. Dodd, *Studies in Stuart Wales* (Cardiff, 1952, 2nd edition, 1971). On the civil war background, principally on the military side, P. Gaunt, *A Nation Under Siege* (London, 1991) is a good, brief introduction.

Much writing on the 1650s has focused on Puritanism, a topic accorded pride of place in Welsh historiography because of the interest in tracing the origins of Welsh nonconformity. The series of books by Thomas Richards, of which *A History of the Puritan Movement in Wales* (London, 1920) is the best known, are marvellous quarries for the researcher, but not to be recommended to those requiring an accessible overview. For that purpose, G. H. Jenkins, *Protestant Dissenters in Wales 1639–1689* (Cardiff, 1992) is ideal, and has an extensive annotated bibliography. A series of lectures by G. F. Nuttall, published as *The Welsh Saints 1640–1660* (Cardiff, 1957), is subtle and full of insights. Nuttall's work has the strengths and weaknesses of having been written by someone fully in sympathy with the religious outlook of his subjects. In similar vein, R. T. Jones, *Vavasor Powell* (Swansea, 1971) provides a Welsh-language biography of one of the principal religious figures in the Principality during the Interregnum.

Many decades of work on the 'Welsh Saints' have provided us with some fine studies of Welsh Puritanism, but other varieties of belief and unbelief in Interregnum Wales have scarcely been studied. The fate of the Anglican church has been studied only as a target of the 'Propagators', and some studies which set Dissent in a wider context or which attempt to portray the experiences of the Welsh in the 1650s in more rounded ways are long overdue.

On government, the collection by Dodd noted above includes a classic study of Welsh committeemen. Tudor innovations and Stuart modifications are a strong suit of J. G. Jones, *Early Modern Wales, c. 1525–1640*

(Cardiff, 1994), athough the reader should note the starting and terminal dates of the book, which do not cover the seventeenth century as a whole. The best study of the leading Welsh politician of the period, Colonel Philip Jones, remains A. G. Veysey, 'Colonel Philip Jones, 1618–74', *Transactions of the Honourable Society of Cymmrodorion* (1966). The biographies of many committeemen, ministers, poets and others may be quarried through *The Dictionary of Welsh Biography*.

On Anglo-Welsh relations, Part 1 of Christopher Hill's *Change and Continuity in 17th Century England* (London, 1974) contains two fine essays on London and the outlying regions, principally Wales, one of which fully explores the concept of the 'dark corners' and Puritan schemes to enlighten them. Interregnum Wales has not been especially well served by county historians, although Philip Jenkins, *The Making of a Ruling Class: The Glamorgan Gentry 1640–1790* (Cambridge, 1983) is a notable exception. See also the important chapter by A. M. Johnson in G. Williams (ed.), *Glamorgan County History*, Vol. iv (Cardiff, 1974); other chapters in that volume contain much relevant material for the study of politics, religion and culture in that county.

An interesting approach to the history of the 1650s in Wales is through its culture, and especially its literature. The works of Morgan Llwyd are of paramount importance in this respect, and may only be fully appreciated by those with some facility in the Welsh language. Nevertheless, M. W. Thomas, *Morgan Llwyd* (Cardiff, 1984) is a good English-language introduction to this fascinating writer. On the opposite side, as it were, in the conflicts of the period was Henry Vaughan, an English-language Welsh poet (the phrase Anglo-Welsh seems no longer to find much approval.) Vaughan is best approached via Alan Rudrum, *Henry Vaughan* (Cardiff, 1981), like Thomas's study of Llwyd, a volume in the University of Wales Press Writers of Wales series. For those with Welsh, *Hen Gerddi Gwleidyddol 1588–1660* (Cymdeithas Llên Cymru ii, Cardiff, 1901) contains ballad material of the period.

Local Government Reform in England and Wales during the Interregnum

For ideas on local government, Mary Cotterell, 'Interregnum Law Reform: The Hale Commission of 1652', *English Historical Review*, 83 (1968), pp. 689–704 and Donald Veall, *The Popular Movement for Law Reform 1640–1660* (Oxford, 1970) are useful surveys, but through W.

Haller and G. Davies (eds), *The Leveller Tracts 1647–1653* (Gloucester, Mass, 1964) readers may trace the development of Leveller views for themselves. See also G. Winstanley, *The Law of Freedom*, ed. Christopher Hill (Harmondsworth, 1973) and Hobbes's *Leviathan*.

On the mechanics of local government Sidney and Beatrice Webb, *English Local Government from the Revolution to the Municipal Corporations Act: The Parish and the County* (London, 1906) should be read with the more recent treatments by, for example, L. M. Hill in C. Russell (ed.), *The Origins of the English Civil War* (London, 1973) and G. C. F. Forster, 'County Government in Yorkshire during the Interregnum', *Northern History*, 12 (1976), pp. 84–104.

Full-length county studies are legion. Of particular interest are A. M. Everitt, *The Community of Kent and the Great Rebellion* (Leicester, 1966); D. Underdown, *Somerset in the Civil War and Interregnum* (Newton Abbot, 1973); J. S. Morrill, *Cheshire 1630–1660: County Government and Society during the English Revolution* (Oxford, 1974); B. G. Blackwood, *The Lancashire Gentry and the Great Rebellion* (Manchester, 1978); and A. Fletcher, *A County Community in Peace and War: Sussex 1600–1660* (London, 1975). Mary Coate, *Cornwall in the Great Civil War and Interregnum 1642–1660* (Oxford, 1933) is a classic. For a Welsh shire see A. M. Johnson, 'Politics and Religion in Glamorgan during the Interregnum' in G. Williams (ed.), *Glamorgan County History*, Vol iv (Cardiff, 1974). Apart from these and other published works cited in the text, Robin Silcock, 'County Government in Worcestershire 1603–1660' (London PhD 1974), Anne Hughes, 'Politics, War and Society in Warwickshire 1620–1660' (Liverpool PhD 1980) and S. K. Roberts, 'Participation and Performance in Devon Local Administration 1649–1670' (Exeter PhD 1980) are among the most recent doctoral theses. Dr Hughes's and Clive Holmes's 'The County Community in Stuart Historiography', *Journal of British Studies*, 19 (1980), pp. 54–73 together offer a substantial modification of what once seemed a consensus on the concept of the 'county community'. A highly original and fruitful approach is that of Keith Wrightson and David Levine in *Poverty and Piety in an English Village: Terling 1500–1700* (Oxford, 1979). G. E. Aylmer and J. S. Morrill (eds), *The Civil War and Interregnum* (London, 1979) is a useful survey of 'sources for local historians'.

Studies of specific local institutions are more difficult to find. J. Morrill, *The Cheshire Grand Jury 1625–59* (Leicester, 1976) and Keith

Wrightson, 'Two Concepts of Order: Justices, Constables and Jurymen in Seventeenth-century England' in J. Brewer and J. Styles (eds), *An Ungovernable People?* (London, 1980) are social interpretations of the local systems of justice. The fortunes of constables may be traced in editions of quarter sessions records, such as that by D. H. Allen for Essex (1974). J. C. Hemmeon, *The History of the British Post Office* (Cambridge, Mass, 1912) is the standard work. See also H. Robinson, *The British Post Office in History* (Princeton, N. J., 1948).

Government policy may be traced in C. H. Firth and R. S. Rait (eds), *Acts and Ordinances of the Interregnum* 3 vols (London, 1911) and in the *Calendars of State Papers Domestic.* On fiscal matters Maurice Ashley, *Financial and Commercial Policy* (Oxford, 1934) is still the only work available.

A recent contribution to the debate on poor relief is the essay on the London workhouse by Valerie Pearl in D. H. Pennington and K. Thomas (eds), *Puritans and Revolutionaries: Essays in Seventeenth Century History Presented to Christopher Hill* (Oxford, 1978).

British Library Add. Ms. 19516, Add. Mss. 34011–17 are the Ms. letter-book and lists of the registered citizens kept by Thomas Dunn and the major-generals. The experience of one county during the period of registration may be assessed in A. R. Bax, 'Suspected Persons in Surrey during the Commonwealth', *Surrey Archaeological Collections*, 15 (1899), pp. 164–89. *The Thurloe State Papers*, ed. T. Birch, 7 vols (1742) are, of course, indispensable. G. E. Aylmer, *The State's Servants* (London, 1973) is primarily a study of bureaucracy but is valuable for its insights into local administration.

Finally, the flavour of the 1650s is conveyed in the diaries and notebooks of county gentlemen who lived through them. See the notebook of Captain John Pickering in *Thoresby Society Publications, Miscellanea iv* and *v* (1904, 1909), the papers of Sir William Boteler in *Bedfordshire Record Society*, 18 (1936), the autobiography of Sir John Gibson, *Surtees Society*, 124 (1915), the edicts of Martin Pyke, JP, and Thomas Delavall, JP, in *Sussex Archaeological Collections*, 20, *Surtees Society*, 84, and the remarkable *Diary of Ralph Josselin* edited by Alan Macfarlane (Oxford, 1976).

POSTSCRIPT

Since the first version of this book was published in 1981, the following are among the more significant works to appear in print.

The theses by Ann Hughes and S. K. Roberts, mentioned above, have been reworked to appear as A. Hughes, *Politics, Society and Civil War in Warwickshire, 1620–1660* (Cambridge, 1987) and S. K. Roberts, *Recovery and Restoration in an English County: Devon Local Administration, 1646–1670* (Exeter, 1985). Another revised doctoral thesis to appear has been A. Coleby, *Central Government and the Localities: Hampshire 1649–1689* (Cambridge, 1987) which covers much more chronological territory after 1649 than Hughes or Roberts. For a commentary on all three, and on other titles in adjacent periods, see D. Hirst, 'Local Affairs in Seventeenth-Century England', *Historical Journal*, 32 (1989).

Since the 1980s, there has been a decline in the number of county studies appearing, and work of a summative kind has appeared, the most notable example being A. Fletcher, *Reform in the Provinces* (New Haven, 1986), which draws very heavily on a wide range of doctoral theses. R. Hutton, *The British Republic 1649–1660* (London, 1990) has 'the centre' and 'the localities' as central to its argument.

On the impact of Puritanism on the localities, D. Hirst, 'The Failure of Godly Rule in the English Republic', *Past and Present*, 132 (1991) is a stimulating essay which takes a pessimistic view of Puritan achievement. Other works on enforcement include Cynthia Herrup, *The Common Peace. Participation and the Criminal Law in Seventeenth-Century England* (Cambridge, 1987), and R. Bennett, 'Enforcing the Law in Revolutionary England: Yorkshire, 1640–1660' (University of London PhD thesis, 1988).

Two essays in the *festschrift* for Ivan Roots bear directly on issues of central and local government relations in the 1650s: A. Fletcher, 'Oliver Cromwell and the Localities: the Problem of Consent', and S. K. Roberts, 'Godliness and Government in Glamorgan', both in C. Jones, M. Newitt and S. Roberts (eds), *Politics and People in Revolutionary England* (Oxford, 1986). A. Fletcher, 'Oliver Cromwell and the Godly Nation' in J. S. Morrill (ed.), *Oliver Cromwell and the English Revolution* (London, 1990) deals with central/local issues but shifts the emphasis away from the secular towards the ecclesiastical. A number of essays in J. S. Morrill (ed.), *Revolution and Restoration. England in the 1650s* (London, 1992) touch on the central and local.

The subject of taxation policy and enforcement has after many years of neglect by historians been addressed very successfully in M. J. Braddick, *Parliamentary Taxation in Seventeenth-Century England*

(Manchester, 1994), which includes chapters on those mainstays of Interregnum finance, the assessment and the excise. The customs, being in origin based on the prerogative of the monarch, are not included in this study.

A new dimension in considering relationships between government and governed was opened up by David Underdown in *Revel, Riot and Rebellion* (Oxford, 1985), which gave popular culture the emphasis it deserved in accounts of the English revolution. The same author's *Fire From Heaven* (London, 1992) is a model study of government in an English town, Dorchester, although it is light on the 1650s.

Oliver Cromwell and his Protectorate Parliaments: Co-operation, Conflict and Control

Biographies of Cromwell abound. Three good, recent studies are the biographies by Barry Coward, *Oliver Cromwell* (Harlow, 1991) and Peter Gaunt, *Oliver Cromwell* (Oxford, 1996) and the collection of essays on different aspects of Cromwell's life and career edited by John Morrill, *Oliver Cromwell and the English Revolution* (Harlow, 1990). The best introduction to the 1650s as a whole, with much on the Protectorate, is Ronald Hutton, *The British Republic 1649–1660* (London, 1990).

There is surprisingly little detailed work on the central government and politics of the Protectorate and less still specifically on the Protectorate parliaments. Despite its age, the great narrative account by S. R. Gardiner, *History of the Commonwealth and Protectorate*, 4 vols (London, 1903), continued by C. H. Firth, *The Last Years of the Protectorate*, 2 vols (London, 1909), remains invaluable. Derek Hirst's essay on Cromwell as Lord Protector in Morrill's *Oliver Cromwell and the English Revolution* is a thoughtful if inevitably brief assessment. Roy Sherwood, *The Court of Oliver Cromwell* (Cambridge, 1977) provides a thorough account of Cromwell's court and household as Protector. Essays by Ivan Roots in Gerald Aylmer (ed.), *The Interregnum* (London, 1972) and in R. H. Parry (ed.), *The English Civil War and After* (London, 1970) examine the ordinances of 1653–4 and the major-generals of 1655–7 respectively.

The personal and public religious issues which shaped so much of the politics of the period are best approached via the essays by J. C. Davis and Anthony Fletcher in Morrill's *Oliver Cromwell and the English*

Revolution, three articles by A. B. Worden—'Toleration and the Cromwellian Protectorate' in W. J. Sheils (ed.), *Persecution and Toleration* (Studies in Church History 21, Oxford, 1984), 'Providence and Politics in Cromwellian England' in *Past and Present*, 109 (1985) and 'Oliver Cromwell and the Sin of Achan' in D. Beales and G. Best (eds), *History, Society and the Churches* (Cambridge, 1985)—and an article by Derek Hirst, 'The Failure of Godly Rule in the English Republic' in *Past and Present*, 132 (1991).

The most detailed work on the strength, influence and political aspirations of the army during the Protectorate is to be found in two, still largely unpublished doctoral theses by Derek Massarella, 'The Politics of the Army, 1647–60' (University of York, 1978) and H. M. Reece, 'The Military Presence in England, 1649–60' (University of Oxford, 1981). Drawing upon Reece, Austin Woolrych argues strongly against seeing the Protectorate as a military dictatorship in 'The Cromwellian Protectorate: A Military Dictatorship?' in *History*, 75 (1990).

The most detailed work on the relative powers of, and the relationship between, the Protector and his Protectorate Council is to be found in a still largely unpublished doctoral thesis by Peter Gaunt, 'The Councils of the Protectorate, from December 1653 to September 1658' (University of Exeter, 1983). However, some of the material, including aspects of the handling of the Protectorate parliaments by Protector and Council, appeared in an article by Gaunt, '"The Single Person's Confidants and Dependants"? Oliver Cromwell and his Protectoral Councillors', *Historical Journal*, 32 (1989).

The seminal work on Cromwell's parliaments, H. R. Trevor-Roper's 1956 article 'Oliver Cromwell and his Parliaments', was subsequently reprinted in several collections, most notably Ivan Roots (ed.), *Cromwell, A Profile* (London, 1973). Roger Howell questioned this interpretation in 'Cromwell and his Parliaments: The Trevor-Roper Thesis Revisited', reprinted in R. C. Richardson (ed.), *Images of Oliver Cromwell* (Manchester, 1993). David L. Smith also offers some thoughts on the same topic in a brief address printed as 'Oliver Cromwell: A Great Parliamentarian?', in *Cromwelliana* (1995). However, the most detailed recent study of the composition and work of the Protectorate parliaments is to be found in a still unpublished doctoral thesis by Sarah Jones, 'The Composition and Activity of the Protectorate Parliaments' (University of Exeter, 1988).

Peter Gaunt, 'Law-Making in the First Protectorate Parliament' in Colin Jones, Malyn Newitt and Stephen Roberts (eds), *Politics and People in Revolutionary England* (Oxford, 1986) and Ivan Roots, 'Lawmaking in the Second Protectorate Parliament' in H. Hearder and H. R. Loyn (eds), *British Government and Administration* (Cardiff, 1974) reassess the two Protectorate parliaments, focusing upon their legislative record, but ranging further afield.

More detailed accounts of specific parliamentary events and developments are to be found in Peter Gaunt, 'Cromwell's Purge? Exclusions and the First Protectorate Parliament', *Parliamentary History*, 6 (1987), T. A. Wilson and F. J. Merli, 'Naylor's Case and the Dilemma of the Protectorate', *University of Birmingham Historical Journal*, 10 (1965–6), and C. H. Firth, 'Cromwell and the Crown', *English Historical Review*, 17 and 18 (1902 and 1903), which remains the most detailed analysis of that episode.

The Politics of the Army and the Quest for Settlement

Accessible source material for army politics can be found in W. C. Abbott (ed.), *Writings and Speeches of Oliver Cromwell*, 4 vols (Cambridge, Mass, 1937–47); T. Birch (ed.), *State Papers of John Thurloe*, 7 vols (1762); C. H. Firth (ed.), *The Clarke Papers*, 4 vols (Camden Society, 1891–1901); J. Rushworth, *Historical Collections*, 7 vols (1659–1701). This can be supplemented by material in the relevant volumes of the *Journal of the House of Commons, Journal of the House of Lords* and *Calendar of State Papers Domestic.*

Sources relating to the army and covering specific aspects of the period can be found in G. R. Bell (ed.), *Memorials of the Civil War: comprising the Correspondence of the Fairfax Family*, 2 vols (1849); G. E. Aylmer (ed.), *The Levellers and the English Revolution* (London, 1975); W. Haller and G. Davies (eds), *The Leveller Tracts 1647–1653* (Gloucester, Mass, 1964); A. L. Morton (ed.), *Freedom in Arms* (London, 1978) on the Levellers; D. M. Wolfe (ed.), *Leveller Manifestoes of the Puritan Revolution* (repr. New York, 1967); B. Taft, 'Voting Lists of the Council of Officers, December 1648', *Bulletin of the Institute of Historical Research*, 52 (1979); A. S. P. Woodhouse, *Puritanism and Liberty*, 3rd edn (London, 1974), covers 1647–9; J. T. Rutt (ed.), *Diary of Thomas Burton*, 4 vols (1828) for the Protectorate parliaments, including Richard Cromwell's; C. H. Firth, 'Cromwell and the Crown', *English Historical*

Review, 83 (1968); F. P. G. Guizot, *History of Richard Cromwell*, 2 vols (1856), esp. the Appendices.

Mention of the army will be found in all the major narratives of the period from S. R. Gardiner onwards and in monographs and articles dealing with related subjects. The founding of the New Model and its politicisation in 1647 are examined from a revisionist perspective in M. Kishlansky, *The Rise of the New Model Army* (Cambridge, 1979). The argument is convincingly challenged in A. Woolrych, *Soldiers and Statesmen* (Oxford, 1987) and I. Gentles, *The New Model Army* (Oxford, 1992). On the New Model's creation, see also C. Holmes, *The Eastern Association* (Cambridge, 1975); A. N. B. Cotton, 'Cromwell and the Self Denying Ordinance', *History*, 61 (1977); M. Kishlansky 'The Case of the Army Truly Stated: The Creation of the New Model Army', *Past and Present, 81 (1978).*

On the events of 1647, including the influence of the Levellers, see also J. S. Morrill, 'Mutiny and Discontent in English Provincial Armies', *Past and Present*, 56 (1972); I. Gentles, 'Arrears of Pay and Ideology in the Army Revolt of 1647' in B. Bond and I. Roy (eds), *War and Society: A Yearbook of Military History* (London, 1975); J. S. Morrill, 'The Army Revolt of 1647' in A. C. Duke and C. A. Tamse (eds), *Britain and the Netherlands, VI: War and Society* (The Hague, 1977); M. Kishlansky, 'The Army and the Levellers: The Roads to Putney', *Historical Journal*, 12 (1979); D. Underdown, 'Honest Radicals in the Counties, 1642–1649' in D. Pennington and K. Thomas (eds), *Puritans and Revolutionaries* (Oxford, 1978); M. Kishlansky, 'Ideology and Politics in the Parliamentary Armies, 1645–9' in John Morrill (ed.), *Reactions to the English Civil War 1642–1649* (London, 1982); J. S. A. Adamson, 'The English Nobility and the Projected Settlement of 1647', *Historical Journal*, 30 (1987).

D. Underdown, *Pride's Purge* (Oxford, 1971) places army politics in 1647–9 within a larger political context. A. Laurence, *Parliamentary Army Chaplains 1642–1651* (Royal Historical Society Studies in History, 59, London, 1990) adds substantially to a neglected but important aspect of the army's history. Aspects of the social history of the army are taken up in C. Carlton, *Going to Wars* (London, 1993).

Published work dealing specifically with army politics in the 1650s remains thin. B. Worden, *The Rump Parliament* (Cambridge, 1974) and A. Woolrych, *Commonwealth to Protectorate* (Oxford, 1982) have much to say about the period 1649–53. B. Taft, 'The Humble Petition of several

Colonels of the Army: Causes, Character and Results of Military Opposition to Cromwell's Protectorate', *Huntington Library Quarterly*, 42 (1978), discusses the Three Colonels' Petition and argues, unconvincingly, that it reflected widespread discontent in the army. Apart from D. W. Rannie, 'Cromwell's Major Generals', *English Historical Review*, 10 (1895), and I. Roots, 'Swordsmen and Decimators: Cromwell's Major Generals' in R. H. Parry (ed.), *The English Civil War and After* (London, 1970), the major-generals remain seriously neglected. A comprehensive analysis of their origins, role and performance is sorely missed. On the collapse of the English Republic and the Restoration of the Stuarts, the best starting point is now R. Hutton, *The Restoration* (Oxford, 1985). See also F. M. S. McDonald, 'The Timing of General George Monck's March into England, 1 January 1660', *English Historical Review*, 105 (1990).

For the units outside England, J. D. St John Seymour, *The Puritans in Ireland 1647–1661* (repr. Oxford, 1961), and T. C. Barnard, *Cromwellian Ireland* (Oxford, 1975) make some reference to the army in Ireland but seriously misrepresent the aims and influence of the Baptist officers. Aspects of army politics in Scotland are treated in F. D. Dow, *Cromwellian Scotland, 1651–1660* (Edinburgh, 1979) and in Flanders in C. H. Firth, 'Royalist and Cromwellian Armies in Flanders 1657–1662', *Transactions of the Royal Historical Society*, new series, 17 (1903). On the navy, see B. Capp, *The Cromwellian Navy* (Oxford, 1989).

Biographies of uneven quality, of some of the most important officers, include M. Ashley, *Cromwell's Generals* (London, 1954); M. Ashley, *General Monck* (London, 1977); J. Berry and S. G. Lee, *A Cromwellian Major General: The Career of Colonel John Berry* (Oxford, 1938); W. H. Dawson, *Cromwell's Understudy: The Life and Times of General John Lambert* (London, 1938); G. E. Lucas Phillips, *Cromwell's Captains* (London, 1938); R. W. Ramsey, *Henry Ireton* (London, 1949); C. H. Simpkinson, *Major General Harrison* (London, 1905); H. G. Tibbutt, 'Colonel John Okey', *Bedfordshire Historical Society*, 35 (1934); J. Wilson, *Fairfax* (London, 1985). Biographies of Oliver Cromwell are legion. But attention may be drawn to G. E. Aylmer, 'Was Oliver Cromwell a Member of the Army in 1646–7 or not?', *History*, 56 (1971); and C. Hoover, 'Cromwell's Status and Pay in 1646–47', *Historical Journal*, 23 (1980).

Index